Put More LEADERSHIP into Your Style

Elwood N. Chapman

 ᴿ

SCIENCE RESEARCH ASSOCIATES, INC.
Chicago, Henley-on-Thames, Sydney, Toronto
An IBM Company

About the Author

Elwood Chapman, lecturer and business training specialist, is perhaps best known as the author of *Your Attitude Is Showing,* one of the most widely used books in the field of business human relations. Mr. Chapman is an experienced teacher (29 years a professor at Chaffey College and 17 years a lecturer at Claremont Graduate School) and a nationally known consultant in the field of retailing. Over the years, Mr. Chapman has written more than a dozen books, most of them reflecting his lifelong interest in the style and substance of the business world.

Other SRA books by the same author:	
College Survival	Your Attitude Is Showing
Career Search	Dynamic Retailing
Career Success	Supervisor's Survival Kit

Library of Congress Cataloging in Publication Data

Chapman, Elwood N.
  Put more leadership into your style.

  1. Leadership. I. Title.
HD57.7.C47 1984   658.4/092   83-16322
ISBN 0-574-20710-4

A Leader's Guide (13-3711) may be ordered from Science Research Associates, Inc., 155 N. Wacker Drive, Chicago, Illinois 60606.

Contents

Exercises

Preface

During the last revision of my book *Supervisor's Survival Kit*, my editors asked me to add a chapter on leadership. They felt that in my eagerness to cover the practical aspects of management I had neglected the concept of leadership.

I did some research and, to my amazement, discovered very little material that would help anyone—especially a supervisor—become a better leader. I found fragments of concepts and theories from sociology, psychology, and political science, and more substantial information in Ralph Stogdill's *Handbook of Leadership* (Free Press, 1974). I also found some excellent leadership articles in journals and periodicals, but there was little that would help me write a short, practical chapter on the fundamentals of leadership.

I eventually finished the chapter, but my interest in the subject was now so intense that I decided to continue my investigation. My sources this time were not books and journal articles on leadership, but the leaders themselves—men and women who exemplified the very qualities and characteristics I wanted to isolate and identify. First, I talked to several successful leaders in my community. On the basis of these early interviews, I constructed a tentative conceptual model (formula), which I then submitted to a second group of men and women who, according to observers, possessed unusual leadership abilities. Each member of the second group (which came from all fields and from all parts of the country) shared ideas and insights with me and encouraged me to continue my investigation into the essence of leadership. Finally, after interviewing numerous corporate executives, educators, coaches, military officers, youth leaders, ministers, and management professors, I felt I had enough material to write this book.

I sincerely thank these men and women for their time and contributions. I would also like to thank the professionals who were kind enough to review this book in manuscript. Their comments and criticism were extremely helpful.

The search for the true nature of leadership will continue long after the publication of the monograph. In the meantime, I believe that the formula presented in this book offers some practical guidelines to those who wish to acquire the skills and behavior patterns associated with successful leadership.

Elwood N. Chapman

There go my people. I must find out where
they are going so I can lead them.

Alexandre Ledru-Rolling
1807–1874

Chapter 1

A Formula for Leadership

A person does not become a leader by virtue of the possession of some combination of traits.

Ralph Stogdill

OBJECTIVES

After finishing this chapter, you will be able to:

• Identify the various parts of the Leadership Formula.

• Evaluate your leadership potential.

To lead. To march at the head of the parade. To win the respect and admiration of your peers. To help others reach worthwhile goals.

If you thought that leadership was beyond your reach, think again. It may not be. Why? First of all, your leadership potential is probably greater than you think it is. (Most people are not aware of—and therefore never realize—their potential for success in many aspects of life.) And second, there are almost as many leadership opportunities as there are potential leaders. Some may be so close to you, you cannot see them.

Think of this book, then, as a road map that will show you the essence of leadership—and as a guide that will help you organize the skills you already have into a marketable leadership package.

DO YOU HAVE THE RIGHT STUFF?

You need not have a particular combination of personality traits to lead others. No one, including psychologists and management experts, has been able to develop a theory which proves that leadership is merely the result of the right combination of personal characteristics. The experts identify so many acceptable traits—and mixes—that almost anybody can qualify. In other words, you are not automatically disqualified as a potential leader because you feel uncomfortable at large parties or because you prefer reading to handball.

This is not to say that you should not make the most of what you have. You should certainly capitalize on your strengths and the positive personality traits you already possess.

The Leadership Potential Scale at the end of this chapter will give you an opportunity to investigate your potential.

WHERE ARE THE LEADERSHIP OPPORTUNITIES?

Everywhere! There are many more leadership opportunities than you suspect. If you think you are ready, there is probably one waiting for you now.

The Upstairs Leadership Dearth Principle states that the farther one goes up the organizational ladder, the harder it is to find people who qualify for the demanding leadership positions at the top. There may be an abundance of leaders at lower levels, but most fall by the wayside before they get close to the top. Some are promoted beyond their level of competency (the Peter Principle) and climb no further; some lose their motivation to become leaders and opt for pure management* roles; and some, those who do rise to the top in the business world, often become so valuable that competitive organizations lure them away.

There are also opportunities and critical needs for leaders in other areas—unions, youth organizations, churches, and community volunteer groups. The leadership crisis you read about is real. And there is no reason why you should not take advantage of it.

THE LEADERSHIP FORMULA

Leadership has always been a nebulous concept. Everyone who has written about it seems to have his or her own explanation or definition. If you are confused about what leadership is, you have plenty of company. We do know that most people who have become successful in leadership roles have done it pretty much on their own, often using other leaders as models.

There is no reason, then, why the same approach will not work for you. To simplify the process, the book presents a prescription, or formula, for increasing your own leadership potential by teaching you how to acquire the common, successful skills, techniques, and principles practiced by men and women who occupy leadership roles in a variety of settings. The formula was not developed merely from reading and observation but was synthesized from the results of interviews with over 60 successful leaders in business, education, sports, religion, youth organizations, politics, and community groups.

The Leadership Formula is presented in graphic form as a multi-leveled pyramid. (See the following page.) Each level represents a different foundation for leadership. Although no one foundation is more important than any other, there is a crescendo or snowball effect as you move from bottom to top. You will also discover that all of the foundations are interrelated, interlocked,

---

*Do not confuse management with leadership. As you will learn in the next chapter, not all managers are leaders.

The Leadership Formula

and interdependent. You will note, too, that the pyramid model encourages you to learn the essence of leadership one step at a time. As far as the order of the steps is concerned, experienced leaders may start anywhere, including the top; beginners, however, should start at the bottom.

Here are some important questions raised by the group of leaders who were kind enough to review this book in manuscript. You may have the same concerns.

PRELIMINARY QUESTIONS AND ANSWERS

Question 1: Will the formula accommodate different leadership styles?

Yes. The object of the formula is to put more leadership into your style, not to change it. A leader who is comfortable with a strong, directive approach can adjust the formula to fit his or her style. So can a leader who believes in, and practices, participatory leadership. Some leaders have a strong human-relations orientation in their style; others are more task-oriented. Some lean more heavily on their personalities than others. It is not necessary to discard one's basic style to adopt the formula. It will fit into all existing comfort zones.

Question 2: Will adopting the formula improve my style?

Definitely. The formula will add substance to any style. Through the adaptation of the formula, one can fill voids, strengthen weak areas, and build further upon strong parts.

Question 3: Some authors use a situational approach to leadership. They seem to say that each environment requires a different kind of leader. Are they wrong?

No. Different situations require different approaches, understandings, sensitivities, and styles. The great advantage to the formula is that it has distilled those basics common to and necessary for success in all situations. It can, therefore, apply as well to a military officer as a politician, a coach as a corporate officer, a minister as a community leader. If a leader moves from one environment to another, certain adjustments to style should be made, but once the formula foundations have been mastered they can be applied to each new situation.

Question 4: Will the formula benefit experienced leaders as well as beginners?

Yes. The difference could be that successful leaders might be content to use the formula to identify one or more weak areas in their style of leadership, whereas beginners might wish to build their complete style around the formula.

Question 5: Is the formula designed for business leaders only?

Absolutely no. It will make sense to those who occupy or hope to occupy any possible leadership role—everything from a student leader in high school to the President of the United States. The formula does, however, incorporate good management practices.

Question 6: Will the formula help produce a better kind of leader for the future?

Yes, because all bases are covered; nothing is left to chance. Properly interpreted and employed, the formula can produce a stronger, more decisive leader and one who is, at the same time, more sensitive to the real needs of followers. This kind of leader is desperately needed at all levels of our society.

As you proceed, keep in mind that the essence of leadership cannot be adequately defined in a single sentence or paragraph. Rather, it is to be found in all the principles presented in the book.

The formula is the message.

Missing Words

Without looking at page 4, write in the key words of the Leadership Formula.

• Most people who want to become successful leaders possess a trait mix that makes it possible.

• Career and volunteer leadership opportunities exist in every setting.

• The Leadership Formula is a practical road map designed to help people at all levels become successful leaders.

• The formula is a composite of successful practices used by leaders in a wide variety of roles.

• The formula (pyramid) is built one foundation at a time.

SUMMARY

Leadership Potential Scale

If you have not had the opportunity to demonstrate your leadership talents, you may have more potential than you think. This scale is designed to help you evaluate just how much potential you possess.

Circle the number that best indicates where you fall in the scale. After you have finished, total your scores in the space provided.

I can develop the confidence to lead others.	10 9 8 7 6 5 4 3 2 1	I could never develop enough personal confidence to lead.
I could set a strong authority line and make it stick.	10 9 8 7 6 5 4 3 2 1	I could not become an authority figure in any situation.
It would not bother me to discipline those under my leadership.	10 9 8 7 6 5 4 3 2 1	I would find it impossible to discipline someone under my leadership.
I can become an outstanding public speaker.	10 9 8 7 6 5 4 3 2 1	I could never become effective at group communication.
I am confident that I would make an excellent decision maker.	10 9 8 7 6 5 4 3 2 1	I do not see myself making decisions that affect others.
I can make hard decisions that would cause others to be upset with me.	10 9 8 7 6 5 4 3 2 1	I don't want anything to do with hard decisions.
It would not bother me to stay aloof from followers.	10 9 8 7 6 5 4 3 2 1	I'd rather be one of the gang.
I am highly self-motivated and seek responsibility.	10 9 8 7 6 5 4 3 2 1	I am not self-motivated; I do not seek responsibility.
I have great compassion for others.	10 9 8 7 6 5 4 3 2 1	I have little or no compassion for others.
I can remain 100% positive in a negative environment.	10 9 8 7 6 5 4 3 2 1	I have a difficult time remaining positive in a positive environment.

TOTAL _____

If you rated yourself 80 or above, it would appear that you have a very high leadership potential. You have the confidence to be a top-flight leader. If you rated yourself between 60 and 80, you have above-average leadership potential. You will probably do well in many leadership roles. If you scored under 60, you may have underrated yourself or you may simply not be ready for a leadership role at this stage of your life. It is suggested that you complete the scale again after you have finished the book.

Keep in mind that the scale is not a scientific instrument; it is nothing more than a self-assessment aid designed to help you measure your own potential for development.

Greg is working toward his MBA degree at night while holding down a management job with a bank during the day. He retired from the military three years ago after twenty years of service. He is 44 years old.

Vicki, a fellow student, is 26. She was an anthropology major in college and is now working as the director of the community's Youth Opportunity program. Vicki has had no previous management training.

During the regular evening break, Greg and Vicki get into a friendly discussion. They are both excited about that night's lecture—on leadership.

"I am convinced," states Greg, "that leadership must be analyzed and understood from a purely situational point of view. Start with the environment first and then build a model. The military requires one kind of leader, business another, and other environments still another. The situation dictates the substance as well as the style. I have had nothing but trouble trying to use my military leadership skills in business. I'm having to start from scratch."

"This is hard for me to accept, Greg," replied Vicki. "If what you say is true then people must wait until they get into a specific environment before building up leadership skills. To me, leadership is leadership. If you learn the essentials in one situation, you can take them with you to another. If you are a general in the army, you can take your leadership capabilities with you into politics. Eisenhower did this. If you are a recognized leader in business, you can take your basic skills with you into education. The real basics or substance of leadership are the same in all environments. Only minor adjustments need to be made to fit the situation, and most of those should be in approach and style. Maybe you didn't learn the real fundamentals in the military and that is why you are having trouble adjusting them to your new environment."

Whom would you support? Why?

(The author's responses to the case studies are given in the back of the book, beginning on page 149.)

Case 1: Conflict

Case 2: Potential

Bob Stark, a candidate for assemblyman in the 25th district, was talking with his campaign manager, Jim Burke, about strategy. The discussion turned to leadership.

"Jim, I agree that leadership is the key to any politician's success, but I also believe that leadership evolves in a natural way and that deliberate attempts at improvement might backfire. My present style is working, so I'm reluctant to add any new components. All it needs is a little polishing. Why tinker with success?"

"I totally disagree, Bob. Polishing your style is good, but there may be some fundamentals of leadership that you have yet to incorporate into your style. Adding just one of them could make a major difference to your political future. I believe that most politicians operate far beneath their leadership potential. They have blind spots in their style. And they keep on making the same old mistakes, trusting to image and exposure to keep them in office."

"Well, Jim, if you feel that my leadership skills need sharpening, then I suppose I could study others and adopt what I like into my style. But nobody can distill the basics of leadership. Nobody can say these are the essentials and these are not. Leadership is not an absolute."

"Sorry, Bob, but there must be a few fundamentals that belong in any style. And you may be jeopardizing your political career because of your tunnel vision."

Do you agree with Bob or Jim? Support your view. (The author's view is given in the back of the book.)

Mark each statement below True or False.

_____ 1. The essential personality traits required for successful leadership have been isolated.

_____ 2. The Upstairs Leadership Dearth Principle states that the higher you get in an organization, the fewer leadership opportunities there are.

_____ 3. Only business leaders have made contributions to the Leadership Formula in this book.

_____ 4. Up until now, most successful leaders have made it on their own.

_____ 5. The foundations in the Leadership Formula are interrelated.

_____ 6. The formula will accommodate all leadership styles, thus making major personality changes unnecessary.

_____ 7. Communication is not a part of the Leadership Formula.

_____ 8. Religious leaders would find it uncomfortable to weave the formula into their style.

_____ 9. The Leadership Formula is designed to add substance to style.

_____ 10. The essence of leadership is the formula itself.

Turn to the back of the book to check your answers.

TOTAL CORRECT _____

Chapter 2

Management Skills—
A Prerequisite for Leadership

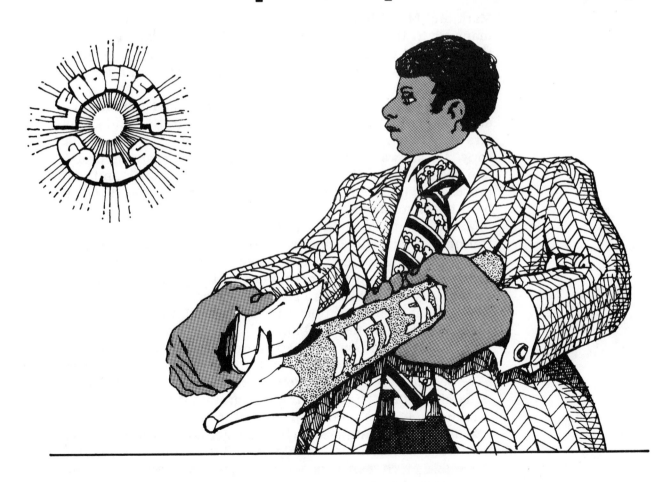

Managers are the maintenance people of business.

Adrian Chalfant, corporation president

OBJECTIVES

After finishing this chapter, you will be able to:

- Explain why management skills are essential to successful leadership.

- List some differences between management and leadership.

- Decide if you are spending too much time on management and not enough on leadership.

Mark and Maria have a lot going for them. He is the new city manager in their community of over 60,000 residents; she is the principal of the local high school. They have an excellent combined income, a lovely home, and both are still under forty years of age.

Mark has built his career on a sound educational foundation — an undergraduate major in Business Administration and a masters in Public Administration. He got his management skills early. He knows how to organize, control, delegate, appraise, and set priorities. He is an expert on public finance and data processing. In recent years he has, on a do-it-yourself basis, been trying to improve his leadership skills.

Maria became a leader without the benefit of management training. First, she demonstrated her leadership ability by heading several faculty committees; then she was appointed chairwoman of her department. Sensing the direction her career was taking, she returned to graduate school to earn a degree in Educational Administration. She now has all the management skills possessed by her husband.

The point is not how or when Mark and Maria got their management training. The important thing is that because they have become efficient managers, they are free to improve their leadership skills. They have the background they need for more demanding leadership roles in the future.

Management training is the best possible foundation on which to build a successful leadership role. But as important as they are, management skills are not a substitute for leadership skills. It is the blend of the two that provides the winning combination.

Writers have been trying for years to explain the difference between management and leadership. It is not an easy task, because the two concepts are so closely interwoven.

MANAGEMENT VERSUS LEADERSHIP

Management is concerned with achieving organizational objectives. Management means communicating, planning, organizing, controlling, and evaluating. It means resolving conflicts. It means setting goals and moving employees toward them.

Management is keeping people productive, maintaining optimal working conditions, and making the best possible use of all resources. Management is anticipating problems and solving them before productivity declines. It is holding things together.

All of these tasks, of course, involve some degree of leadership. But leadership is not synonymous with management.

A manager may develop the perfect strategy to make an organization successful, but unless he or she is also a leader, the strategy will fail. Leadership, then, takes a bigger, broader view. Leadership takes you into new territory. As a manager, you may be content to work primarily inside the framework of your organization; as a leader you become increasingly concerned with the direction the organization itself is taking. As a manager, you may be satisfied to follow the lead of high-level personnel; as a leader you prepare yourself to become a member of the group that leads.

As a leader, you still manage but you add a new dimension to your responsibilities. You start to change your image from a maintenance person to a mover, from a data giver to a data user, from a decision follower to a decision maker. The transition from pure management to leadership may appear to be subtle, but when it happens, it doesn't take long for others to notice the change.

Your concept of leadership will continue to grow and change as you proceed through this book. Slowly you will sense other differences between management and leadership. The Leadership Formula graphic shows the management function running parallel to the foundations of leadership. This was done to remind you that management skills will help you make the most of the Leadership Formula. Spillovers between management and leadership occur. And no matter how far you cross over in the direction of pure leadership, you will never get completely away from management.

An Exercise in Association

Quickly, without referring to what you have just read, write the first words that come to mind when you think of the following terms.

Management: _____

_____

Leadership: _____

_____

Did you use some of the same terms to describe both words? Or did your choices indicate that the two concepts are clearly separated in your mind? It might be interesting to ask a friend to do this exercise with you or, if you are reading the book in a group situation, to discuss your responses with your fellow students.

NOT ALL MANAGERS WANT TO MAKE THE TRANSITION TO LEADERSHIP

Grace and Cynthia were owners of a thriving interior design business with seven locations. They were both good managers. One day Grace told Cynthia that she had been nominated for president of the national trade association to which they both belonged. Cynthia replied: "Go ahead. Tell them you'd like the job. I'm doing okay as a manager, and that's all I want to be. You are the one who will enjoy being a leader, and you'll be good at it."

Cynthia has learned that some individuals are happier as managers. It is not difficult to find people like Cynthia, capable individuals who at one time aspired to be leaders, but are now satisfied to ride out their management roles.

Bank President: "Many of our successful, irreplaceable managers are just not interested in a more demanding leadership position. It is easier and safer to stay a manager."

Utility Executive: "We've had some outstanding managers who tried to become leaders and washed out. They made the mistake of thinking that leadership is no more than an extension of management."

There is an interesting twist to the entire management-leadership dichotomy.

> YOU CAN BE AN EXCELLENT MANAGER WITHOUT BECOMING
> A GOOD LEADER. BUT YOU CANNOT BE AN EXCELLENT LEADER
> WITHOUT BECOMING A GOOD MANAGER.

For the most part, the above statement is true. Good management skills provide not only the foundation for good leadership but also (in most cases) the time to lead. You simply cannot become a strong leader until the management side of the operation is running smoothly.

Making the transition from a management position requires commitment. Even for experienced managers, acquiring new leadership skills is not an overnight proposition. Why? One reason is that leadership is really a state of mind. You must want to become a leader before changes can occur. A second, more powerful reason is the management marshmallow.

Managing a firm, a department, a team, a school, or a government agency always involves a mass of details. There are procedures to follow, reports to write, controls to cross-check. Administrative work is not always exciting, but it is necessary. How else can plans be implemented and productivity measured? Frequently, however, managers permit themselves to become so immersed in managerial functions that they cannot see the leadership "forest" for the management "trees." Administrative work can draw managers deeper and deeper into the management marshmallow—the soft, comfortable, gooey cloud of detail that keeps them from seeing the big picture.

To lead, one must look beyond the familiar pleasures of routine work. Unfortunately, some managers are unable to do so.

The Upward Mobility Leadership Expansion Principle states that those who want to move up must *reduce* the time spent on administrative matters and *expand* the time devoted to leadership. The theory implies that those who fail to make the transition into leadership fast enough may be passed over. Generally speaking, beginning supervisors should devote the vast majority of their time to management activities. But when they move into the next level of management, the reverse should be true. Leadership ability, not management ability, is the primary criterion for a continued upward mobility.

A corollary to this theory: The sooner an individual demonstrates leadership skills at the bottom of the ladder, the sooner he or she begins to move up; the longer that person waits, the more likely it is that he or she will be left behind in a minor management role.

LEADERS WITHOUT MANAGEMENT TRAINING MUST LEARN THE HARD WAY

Most people move into leadership roles from management positions—but not all. Some make the transition from positions as homemakers, students, and community volunteers. These individuals do not have to fight the management marshmallow problem, but in order to survive, they need to learn management skills as they go along. Learning how to delegate, set priorities, manage time, and so on, must be mastered at the same time they are incorporating leadership skills into their style. It is a double responsibility. Here is the way the director of athletics at a large college views the problem: "I'm glad I was a successful coach before I took over this job because I was able to develop most of my leadership skills before I arrived. But I have learned to respect management skills. My transition would have been much easier if I had taken some management courses earlier."

TIME DEVOTED TO MANAGEMENT VERSUS LEADERSHIP

Interviewing top leaders gave me an opportunity to ask them how much time they spend on the two functions. Only two stated firmly that virtually all of their time was devoted to leadership efforts. A few indicated that a majority of their time was spent on what they termed leadership matters, but most said that they devoted far more time to management than leadership.

The most interesting finding, however, was that all wanted to free themselves to spend more time on leadership. One president of a major firm in Boston stated: "I doubt that I spend even half of my time on leadership matters, but it isn't because I don't want to. I find there are always fires for me to put out; usually problems that my managers can't handle. This means I must put on my management hat and continue to wear it until things are squared away. You might interpret this to be a reflection on my lack of leadership ability, but I believe it is something all corporate heads must deal with."

Ideally, leaders at the very top should spend about 20 percent of their time on management and 80 percent on leadership. Reality, of course, can dictate otherwise. The percentage of time

---

Management Skills Checklist

This exercise is designed to provide those of you who have had limited management training with a brief look at the kinds of skills that, if mastered, will free you to lead. Place a checkmark next to those areas in which you feel competent.

☐ Budgeting

☐ Preparing financial statements

☐ Delegating work

☐ Creating and maintaining a good working climate

☐ Appraising results

☐ Preparing production quotas, sales plans, etc.

☐ Analyzing computer data

☐ Setting priorities—personal and organizational

☐ Managing your time

☐ Interpreting statistical data

☐ Planning and control

☐ Resolving conflict

---

devoted to leadership gradually drops for those in less responsible positions. This should not be interpreted to mean that first-line managers should be satisfied with the limited time they spend on leadership. They should constantly strive for more, keeping in mind that the better they are at management, the more time they have free to devote to leadership.

A FEW SUCCESSFUL LEADERS REMAIN POOR MANAGERS

Just as we have excellent managers with little leadership ability, we have some leaders who are weak managers. Some are so good at leadership that their lack of management skills is overlooked. This is especially true in nonbusiness environments. It is possible to lead a regiment, run a Girl Scout troop, or coach a Little League team without being a superior manager. The management function in many situations is minimal. Some leaders (politicians, film producers, coaches) may be so good that their poor management skills can be ignored or at least tolerated. There are also cases where the powers that be will provide a good manager to act as a backstop for an exceptional leader. Good leaders are much harder to find than good managers. And managers are paid less.

Still, any leader who is not also a good manager is always vulnerable. Poor organization will undermine the leader's authority and may eventually contribute to his or her collapse. As much as subordinates may value a particular person's leadership qualities, they still like to work or play in a nonchaotic environment.

It always works both ways.

Successful leaders without adequate management skills should protect themselves by enrolling in a management training program; successful managers who wish to become more than administrators should avail themselves of any leadership training available.

One complements the other.

SUMMARY

- Management skills constitute the best possible background for successful leadership; they should never be neglected.

- Management skills, however, do not replace leadership skills.

- You can be an excellent manager without becoming a good leader, but (except in a few cases) you cannot be an excellent leader without becoming a good manager.

- Managers can increase their chances for upward mobility by devoting more time to their leadership skills.

- Successful leaders who are short on management skills can protect their careers with additional management training.

Making the Transition

Individuals steeped in management techniques often have trouble moving into the more rarified atmosphere of leadership. The management marshmallow is a handicap. Regardless of where you are coming from, this exercise is designed to give you an indication of how difficult the transition may be for you. For best results, match and discuss your results with someone else who has completed the exercise.

I'm more people- than task-oriented.	10 9 8 7 6 5 4 3 2 1	I'm more task- than people-oriented.
I'm a risk-taker.	10 9 8 7 6 5 4 3 2 1	I always play it safe.
Leadership—stepping out in front—is more satisfying than management.	10 9 8 7 6 5 4 3 2 1	Management—paying attention to detail—is more satisfying than leadership.
I like to speak out.	10 9 8 7 6 5 4 3 2 1	I prefer to let my work speak for me.
I welcome change.	10 9 8 7 6 5 4 3 2 1	I like predictability.
I'd rather make tough decisions than accumulate the data.	10 9 8 7 6 5 4 3 2 1	I'd rather submit the data on which decisions are made.
I love to speak to large groups.	10 9 8 7 6 5 4 3 2 1	Give me a back seat, please.
Working with computers and data does little for me.	10 9 8 7 6 5 4 3 2 1	Data analysis and control intrigues me.
Research is not for me.	10 9 8 7 6 5 4 3 2 1	I love research, especially preparation of reports.
I believe management is a subcategory of leadership.	10 9 8 7 6 5 4 3 2 1	I believe leadership is a subcategory of management.

TOTAL _____

If you rated yourself 80 or above, the transition into a leadership position should be easier for you than most. If you rated yourself under 60, the transition might be more difficult.

Case 3: Controversy

Professor Adams is the highly respected dean of the Business School at the state university. He has written three management books. His faculty is considered the most capable and experienced in the Northwest, Two years ago Dr. Adams submitted a request to the curriculum committee to instigate a new course in Leadership for all students on campus. The committee finally approved the request, but Dr. Rosen, dean of instruction, does not feel the course should be taught in the Business School. He argues; "I believe management professors, no matter how capable, are so far into the management forest that they cannot see the leadership trees. I'm not sure they can treat the subject objectively. After all, we need political, community, and religious leaders every bit as much as we need good business leaders. If we offer the course in the Social Science department, we will attract more students from these disciplines. There is, as you know, a great need to train our own student leaders on this campus. I doubt if many of them would enroll in a business course."

Dr. Adams is most upset by this turn of events. His counter-arguments are:

"A good management background is essential to good leadership. They cannot be separated. I believe I have two or three professors who could do an outstanding job of teaching the subject. They already know management and they have been dealing with the subject of leadership in their courses. Professors in the Social Science area, without a management background, would be at a serious disadvantage. Students preparing for nonbusiness leadership roles will benefit immeasurably from the management orientation they will receive. I can guarantee you that we will deal effectively with the subject of leadership in all areas of society. The course would not have, as Dr. Rosen implies, a 100 percent business orientation."

Whom would you support in the controversy? What other arguments would you submit from either side? Why, in your opinion, do many colleges neglect the important subject of leadership? (For the author's reactions, turn to the back of the book.)

Samantha and her husband, Elgin, frequently discuss their careers and their futures over after-dinner coffee. Elgin, an MBA, is a middle manager in a large oil company. Although bored with the job he now holds (because it does not make use of his capabilities), Elgin believes that his training in management theory will eventually spring him into a high-level leadership position with his firm.

Case 4: Opinion

Samantha is a successful high school coach. Her basketball and softball teams have won state championships. She is also president of the local teachers association. She feels that she has already mastered much of what there is to know about leadership. She also believes that her leadership experiences constitute the best possible launching pad into an administrative role. At Elgin's suggestion, she is currently taking her first course in management at a local college.

"Elgin, I believe I have a real edge on the others in my class who are also seeking administrative positions. I think my record as a successful leader puts me at a definite advantage. As soon as I get a few management techniques under my belt, I'm ready to move. I won't have to learn leadership techniques once I get my first administrative opportunity."

"You'd be better off, Sam, if you had more management expertise before you moved into leadership. Management is the foundation of leadership. You've got the cart before the horse. Right now you are underestimating the importance of management and overestimating what you know about leadership. I suggest you get a degree in management, and then perhaps some of your leadership experience will give you a slight advantage."

"Come off it, Elgin. You have been so brainwashed by your management training that you can't think straight. You talk management, management, management, until I'm tired of it. You never even use the word leadership. You don't even know what it means. I'm already a leader, so I will never fall so deeply into the management trap that I'll lose sight of what organizations really need. If you really knew what I'm talking about you would not be boxed into that position you hate."

Whom do you feel has the best background for future success? Elgin with his excellent management foundation or Samantha with her leadership experiences? Defend your position. (The author's views are listed in the back of the book.)

Self-Test   Mark each statement below True or False.

_____ 1. Management is not an integral part of the Leadership Formula.

_____ 2. Management skills constitute part of the substance clearly needed to back up a successful leadership style.

_____ 3. Management skills are not a substitute for leadership skills.

_____ 4. Those who aspire to be leaders, but do not have management backgrounds, can learn management techniques along with leadership skills.

_____ 5. You can become an excellent manager and not be a good leader.

_____ 6. You must be in upper management before you can put more leadership in your style.

_____ 7. The Upward Mobility Leadership Expansion Principle says that those seeking to move higher in their organizations should reduce the time spent on administrative matters and expand the time devoted to leadership.

_____ 8. Some successful leaders are poor managers.

_____ 9. Leaders can never get completely away from their management responsibilities.

_____ 10. Good managers are in a better position than poor managers to free themselves to lead.

Turn to the back of the book to check your answers.

TOTAL CORRECT _____

Chapter 3

Become a Better Communicator

Communication is something so simple and difficult that we can never put it in simple words.

T. S. Mathews

OBJECTIVES

After finishing this chapter, you will be able to:

• View yourself more objectively as a communicator.

• Know what areas of communication you must improve to reach your leadership potential.

Communication is the number-one foundation in the leadership pyramid. And it should be. It is the glue that holds our Leadership Formula together.

Verbal and nonverbal communication keeps leader-follower relationships alive and healthy. Leaders must be better communicators than their subordinates. They must be perceptive listeners, experts at one-on-one conversation, students of small-group dynamics, and outstanding speakers and writers.

How do you rate yourself as a communicator?

The Leadership Communication Scale on the following page will help you assess your present communication skills.

One way to be more objective about your communication skills is to have another person rate you on the same scale, and then compare the two scores. (A duplicate scale is provided on page 163.) The person you select should be one who is concerned about your future and one who is in a position to observe your present communication skills.

Regardless of where you stand at this point, you can show immediate improvement in the following five vital areas of communication.

LEADERS MUST BECOME SUPERIOR LISTENERS

Leaders need to be good listeners because unless they know what their followers want, they will not know where to lead them.

Followers have little radar sets that are constantly tuned into their leaders. Followers know when they are being listened to and when they are being tuned out. When they no longer believe their leader hears them, they start looking for a new one.

Conversations with followers will usually bring comments similar to these to the surface:

"I don't think my leader is as good at listening as she thinks she is."

Leadership Communication Scale

Circle the number that best indicates where you fall in the scale, and enter the total in the space at the bottom.

I am constantly aware of my communication responsibilities.	10 9 8 7 6 5 4 3 2 1	I need to be reminded over and over about the importance of communication.
I understand fully the importance of nonverbal communication. I always project an outstanding visual image.	10 9 8 7 6 5 4 3 2 1	I constantly need to be reminded that there is such a thing as nonverbal communications. People must accept me the way I am.
I have learned how to keep my audience's attention when I talk to any size group.	10 9 8 7 6 5 4 3 2 1	The moment I start to talk I sense people are taking their minds elsewhere.
Rate me a 10 as a listener. I have developed all the skills and I practice them.	10 9 8 7 6 5 4 3 2 1	Give me a 1. I am a terrible listener.
I know how to adjust my conversation to the vocabulary and interest levels of others.	10 9 8 7 6 5 4 3 2 1	I always seem to be talking to myself.
I use appropriate voice control, diction, and delivery techniques.	10 9 8 7 6 5 4 3 2 1	I've given up on becoming even an average public speaker.
I seem to be able to pick just the right words to convey my message.	10 9 8 7 6 5 4 3 2 1	I'm clumsy with words. I'm always putting my foot in my mouth.
My messages are clear, concise, and extremely well received.	10 9 8 7 6 5 4 3 2 1	If I get any feedback at all, it is bad.
I never over- or under-talk; I'm always on target.	10 9 8 7 6 5 4 3 2 1	I either say too much or too little.
I instinctively know which media to use, and I fully employ all communications systems available.	10 9 8 7 6 5 4 3 2 1	Not only do I fail to use the right media, I do not take advantage of the opportunities available.

TOTAL _____

If you rated yourself 80 or above, you appear to possess outstanding communication skills. If you rated yourself between 60 and 80, you may be getting a signal that some improvement is necessary if you are to reach your leadership potential. If you rated yourself under 60, it would appear that substantial improvement is necessary.

"I have, when possible, walked away from leaders who failed to consult me."

"Leaders unseat themselves when they make the mistake of listening to a few close followers and ignoring the rest of us."

Ask Yourself These Questions

	Yes	No
Do I listen as well as I speak?	☐	☐
Do I allow subordinates to express their thoughts without interruptions?	☐	☐
Do I know what my followers (or friends) are really thinking?	☐	☐
Do I have a reputation among my colleagues as a good listener?	☐	☐

In your quest to become a better leader, write in the box below the percentage improvement you would like to achieve in your listening skills.

%

LEADERS MUST BE EXPERTS AT ONE-ON-ONE COMMUNICATION

Good leaders know when to be quiet listeners. They also know when to be engaging conversationalists. They know how to start up informal, one-on-one conversations in any environment. They are experts at dissipating psychological barriers between themselves and their followers. They are perceptive in the questions they ask; they are skilled in the way they ask them.

In only a few moments, a good leader can introduce an important subject, communicate a goal, and reinforce a relationship with a subordinate who may have been neglected or who may have been headed in the wrong direction. A good leader has a way of gaining attention, conveying a message, and leaving a subordinate with the sense that he or she had been a full partner in the dialogue. When successful leaders circulate, they leave a wake of newly challenged followers behind them.

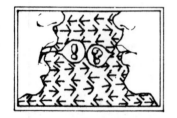

When successful leaders counsel their subordinates, they practice the 5 R's of communication.

RIGHT PURPOSE: They counsel only when there is high probability it will improve the leader-subordinate relationship.

RIGHT TIMING: They counsel only when the mood on both sides appears appropriate.

RIGHT PLACE: They select private locations where there will be few interruptions and the subordinate's privacy is protected.

RIGHT APPROACH: They are nonthreatening in their approach.

RIGHT TECHNIQUE: When they are forced to discipline subordinates, they also inspire them to improve.

Ask Yourself These Questions

	Yes	No
Do people enjoy private conversations with you to the point that they seek you out?	☐	☐
Can you quickly establish a nonthreatening conversational climate with a subordinate?	☐	☐
Can you give subordinates the impression they have done 50 percent of the talking even if they have not?	☐	☐
Can you, through a single private conversation, convert a disenchanted subordinate into a disciple?	☐	☐

Write out the percentage of improvement you would like to see in your one-on-one communications.

☐ %

Successful leaders have the capacity to develop an inner circle of staff people who are loyal and competent. A good leader's staff becomes an extension of his or her own image or leadership style. Good communication skills help to create, and maintain, the close bond between a leader and his staff.

LEADERS MUST BE STUDENTS OF SMALL-GROUP DYNAMICS

Dr. Lockwood's colleagues could not figure out why her students were so enthusiastic about her seminars at the university. Was it her youth and style? Her command of her subject? If asked, Dr. Lockwood's students would have talked about her touch in working with small groups—her ability to draw a reluctant student into a discussion, her skill at turning a hostile student's response into a statement the group could deal with positively, her competency at sensing and articulating the underlying meaning and mood of group discussions. Most of all, they would have mentioned how she used just the right amount of leadership to keep the group on track without stifling creativity.

A leader must be tuned into the dynamics of small groups. He or she must know how to facilitate consensus and at the same time improve relationships with all those involved. This is not an easy task. Still, a leader who cannot function well in a small-group setting is severely handicapped.

Ask Yourself These Questions

	Yes	No
Are you relaxed, comfortable, and effective when leading a small-group discussion?	☐	☐
Can you perceive and communicate group thinking patterns back to the members, so that the best decision is made?	☐	☐
Can you convert a complacent group into a group headed in the right direction but not so much that it might discourage contributions from one or more members?	☐	☐

What percentage of improvement would you like to see in your small-group communication skills?

%

All highly successful leaders—coaches, ministers, community leaders, corporate executives, and politicians—eventually become small-group communication experts. Many take special seminars early in their development to enhance these skills.

All leaders, sooner or later, have opportunities to speak to large groups. The way they handle this task has a great impact on their future success. Their goal should be to build better relationships with current followers and to create new ones.

LEADERS MUST BECOME ACCOMPLISHED SPEAKERS

Ask Yourself These Questions

	Yes	No
Do you have enough confidence to speak to large audiences?	☐	☐
Are you good at audience analysis?	☐	☐
Are you skillful at receiving, interpreting, and answering difficult questions in large groups?	☐	☐
After speaking to a sizable group, do you feel good about yourself and your speaking skills?	☐	☐

Write the percentage improvement you would like to see in your large-group speaking skills.

%

Few leaders are in a position to employ professional ghost writers. (Although some may hide behind the skills of a gifted secretary or assistant.) Most must rely on their own competencies. They must, word by word, sentence by sentence, write their own letters, bulletins, and memos to people outside and inside the organization. They must make sure their written messages will grab the reader's attention, carry the message they wish to convey, will not be misinterpreted, and are free from errors.

A leader who sends out poorly written messages will not be a leader for long. Subordinates want their leader's messages to

LEADERS CANNOT AFFORD TO NEGLECT THEIR WRITING SKILLS

reflect his or her leadership style. They want powerful and decisive messages. If the messages are not, the absence of the leader's stamp is quickly noted.

Ask Yourself These Questions

	Yes	No
Are you proud of your writing skills?	☐	☐
Do your writing skills command as much attention and response as your verbal skills?	☐	☐
Do you use the telephone to avoid writing messages even when the printed form is more effective?	☐	☐
Do you depend too much on the writing skills of others to protect your own leadership image?	☐	☐

Write, in the space below, the percentage of improvement you would like to show in your written communications.

☐ %

The first step to take in putting more leadership into your style is to improve your personal communication skills in all areas. If this means going back to school to take special courses in communications, including public speaking, do it. If you feel you can do it yourself, start now.

Good communication is the heart of leadership.

- Leaders must be above-average communicators.

- Nonverbal communication is as critical as verbal.

- Leaders must be superior listeners to know what followers are thinking.

- Through sensitive one-on-one conversations, leaders can convert reluctant followers into disciples.

- Understanding small-group dynamics can help a leader build a loyal, supportive staff.

- Leaders need to be good at public speaking.

- Writing skills should not be neglected.

SUMMARY

Leadership Comparison Exercise—An Introduction

As mentioned earlier, successful leaders in the past tended to model themselves after other leaders they admired. This was the only path open to those who wished to guide their own leadership growth. Today we call this process "behavioral modeling," and some management experts still believe that modeling is the best, or only, way to acquire leadership skills.

This exercise introduces another measure of leadership.

You are invited to select as your models three leaders you respect and evaluate their leadership ability in each area covered by the five foundations of the Leadership Formula— step by step as you proceed through the book. In this way you will be able to rate your models according to specific behavioral criteria. In other words, you will be looking at substance, not style.

This assessment exercise has two goals. First, it will permit you to verify that each foundation is an essential part of leadership. (And, not incidentally, it will also convince you of the importance of the foundations and motivate you to integrate them into your own behavior.) Second, the exercise will give you a useful yardstick by which you can assess the leaders in your own life—your boss, your congressional representative, your President.

Please follow these steps.

STEP 1: After careful thought, select the leader you respect most in your work or school environment. If you are with an organization, profit or nonprofit, you might consider the president or perhaps a leader closer to you. It is vital that you have the opportunity to observe this individual's leadership behavior

Leadership Comparison Exercise—An Introduction
(*continued*)

        fairly closely. If you do not work (or have no opportunity to observe a leader in your academic environment), observe the behavior of a president of a local or national organization you are familiar with. Write the name of the individual you have chosen in the appropriate blank below. Do this now.

STEP 2:   Do the same for the political world. The person you choose can be anyone from the President of the United States to your mayor. Write this individual's name in the blank provided.

STEP 3:   Select a third respected leader from another environment. Your choice could be a coach, a minister, a youth or community leader. Here again, make sure you have (or have had) an opportunity to observe the behavior of this person closely. If your first two choices were of the same sex, try to select someone from the opposite sex for your third choice. Write down the name.

   1. Working environment model: *Fred Hanson*

   2. Political model: *Mark Hatfield*

   3. Community model: *Mildred Schwab*

The selections you have made are critical because you will continue to evaluate these models in future exercises. At the end, you will make a composite comparison of all three.

   Now turn the page, and complete the first exercise.

Leadership Comparison Exercise—Communication

You are now ready to rate your three models as communicators. Compare their demonstrated communication skills from a leadership angle. Using the chapter as a guide, make the comparisons from your position as a subordinate and/or admirer. In doing this, ask yourself these questions:

- Does this leader keep group members informed?
- Do you want to listen to this leader?
- Is a sense of strength transmitted through her or his voice?
- Does this leader communicate well both nonverbally and verbally?
- Have you ever been disappointed by this leader's ability to communicate?

The model you rate number 1 below (do this now) should be a measurably better communicator than the models you rank 2 and 3. The model you rate number 3 should be measurably weaker than numbers 1 and 2. Once you have completed your ratings, justify them by writing in as many strong and weak points as possible.

	Strong Points	Weak Points
Number 1 _____ (best communicator)		
Number 2 _Mark Hatfield_	_good speaker_ _communicates well_	_small scandal_
Number 3 _Ron Mehl_	_people listen_ _good stories that relate_	

Personal Communication Survey
(optional)

The communication survey on the following page will make you more aware of your strengths and weaknesses as a communicator. Please follow these instructions.

1. Reproduce as many questionnaires as you wish but do not settle for less than three. (Three extra copies are provided on pages 165–69.)

2. Distribute them only to individuals who know you well, will take the survey seriously, and will be fair and honest in their responses.

3. Give each person an envelope so that he or she can return the results sealed inside.

4. Give all sealed envelopes to another person, one who has offered to summarize the results for you on a separate piece of paper (or a clean copy of the questionnaire form) so that you will not know the identity of any single individual.

5. Once you have evaluated the results, make a serious contract with yourself to improve.

Communications Survey Questionnaire

Dear co-worker, colleague, friend, or fellow student:

I have made a contract with myself to become a better communicator. I am asking you for assistance. Please complete the following survey, basing your ratings on the communications we have had in the past. First, rate me on both the listening and speaking scale (between 10, the best rating, and 1, the worst). Second, place a check in any box you think is applicable. Your criticisms will help me improve my skills. You are also encouraged to write out any suggestions for improvement not covered in the questionnaire.

Once you have finished, place this form in the envelope I have provided and seal it. I will, in turn, give your envelope (along with others) to a third person, who will provide me with a summary sheet. Your anonymity will be protected.

LISTENING SKILLS		SPEAKING SKILLS	
High 10 9 8 7 6 5 4 3 2 1 Low		**High** 10 9 8 7 6 5 4 3 2 1 Low	
Suggestions for improvement:		*Suggestions for improvement:*	
Refrain from interrupting so much.	☐	Speak more softly.	☐
Be less defensive when you reply.	☐	Speak with more authority.	☐
Slow your mind down so that you won't anticipate what I say before I say it.	☐	Speak more clearly.	☐
Let me know you are listening by more frequent eye contact.	☐	Speak less but say more.	☐
Improve your concentration.	☐	Put more excitement into your voice.	☐
Other suggestions: _____		Other suggestions: _____	

Bettina Blake has, for some time, been debating in her own mind whether or not to strengthen her communications skills by taking a formal course in public speaking. She has been told by her close friends that although she has a natural ability as a speaker, she should take a course to sharpen her skills. But every time a course is offered, Bettina backs away from making a decision. She rationalizes that she can become better without formal help.

Yesterday she was invited to speak to over 500 people at a convention next spring. She accepted, knowing it would be her biggest, most important audience ever. The talk will be critical to her leadership image. In making her plans, she figures she has three possibilities as far as improving her skills is concerned.

Case 5: Improvement

1. Use her video tape as a tool to improve her speaking ability on a do-it-yourself basis.
2. Take a formal course in public speaking. Ample time remains.
3. Rely on her natural ability, but get as much actual experience in front of groups of all sizes before the big day arrives.

Which of the above strategies do you feel would provide Ms. Blake with the most help? Second? Third? If you were in her shoes what additional experiences would you seek? (The author's rankings are given in the back of the book.)

Matthew Morrison is a campaign adviser to politicians. When his clients appear before large groups, Matt constantly reminds them that they should expand their visual exposure and reduce their verbal exposure. Matt becomes upset if a candidate speaks more then ten minutes. He also counsels his clients to keep their media messages short and to the point. He frequently tells them to make each speech half as long as the audience expects it to be. He encourages all his clients to go to a more expensive tailor.

Case 6: Exposure

If you were a political candidate, would you accept Matt's advice? (The author's response is given in the back.)

Self-Test Mark each statement below True or False.

_____ 1. To be successful, leaders must be measurably better at communication than their followers.

_____ 2. Nonverbal communication is more important than verbal.

_____ 3. Most leaders should delegate their writing responsibilities to others.

_____ 4. Followers cannot tell whether or not their leaders are listening.

_____ 5. Communication is the glue that holds the Leadership Formula together.

_____ 6. A person who scores below 60 on the Leadership Communication Scale could never be a leader.

_____ 7. Leaders who are poor listeners often lose their followers without knowing why.

_____ 8. The 5 R's refer to public-speaking techniques.

_____ 9. Immediate staff members should be an extension of the leader's leadership style.

_____ 10. The foundation of the leadership pyramid is good management skills.

Turn to the back of the book to check your answers.

TOTAL CORRECT _____

Chapter 4

Use the Mutual Reward Theory to Increase Your Following

Leadership is a process of mutual stimulation which, by the interplay of individual differences, controls human energy in the pursuit of a common goal.

P. Pigors, 1935

OBJECTIVES

After finishing this chapter, you will be able to:

• Explain how the Mutual Reward Theory works.

• List some personal and general rewards you want to provide your followers.

It stands to reason that a leader cannot be a leader without followers. But where do followers come from? And assuming you find any, how do you get them to accept you as their leader?

One way to acquire a following is to practice the Mutual Reward Theory.

If you have ever observed two monkeys grooming each other at the zoo, you have seen the Mutual Reward Theory (MRT) operating at its most basic level. When MRT works, both parties come out ahead. In the case of the monkeys, they both have something done for them that they cannot do effectively by themselves. Their lives are thereby enhanced.

Your first reaction may be that MRT is no more than a truism, just another restatement of the old human-relations principle: "If you scratch my back, I'll scratch yours."

When it comes to leadership, it is much more.

MRT states that a relationship between two people (or groups) is improved and enhanced when there is a satisfactory exchange of rewards between them. It is upon this human-relations principle that all leader-follower relationships are built. Unless both parties (leader and follower) come out ahead, the relationship will not last. MRT is, therefore, one of the irreplaceable foundations of the Leadership Formula.

Receiving the right rewards makes followers want to follow. When followers follow with enthusiasm, leaders want to continue to lead. The following syllogism states the concept in a different way.

People who want to lead must have followers.

Followers support people who provide rewards.

Therefore, people who want to become leaders must provide rewards.

Model A shows a typical reward exchange. It is less than ideal because the followers provide more rewards than the leader. Under this reward system, followers follow reluctantly.

ILLUSTRATIONS OF REWARD EXCHANGES

Model B illustrates a better exchange mix; both parties give and receive about the same number of rewards. The balance bar is closer to the middle. In an ideal system not only are the rewards somewhat equally distributed, but they are the right ones—those that each party seeks. Under this reward system, followers follow with vigor and spirit.

When you provide more and better rewards you put more leadership into your style.

GOOD LEADERS PROVIDE PRIMARY REWARDS

Leaders employ their listening skills to search out the "hot buttons," the rewards that followers *really* want (not those that the leaders *think* they want, or should have).

A single, highly prized reward is sometimes more valuable than a number of less important rewards. For example, in a city council election, voters might place a much greater value on better police protection than any other issue in the campaign. Police protection, therefore, becomes the primary reward; it overshadows other less important, possible rewards (better schools, more senior citizen facilities). The candidates who promise better police protection, then, will receive the voters' support.

Missing Rewards

List three rewards your present leader could easily provide but has not done so.

1. _____

2. _____

3. _____

GOOD LEADERSHIP ITSELF IS A VALUED PRIMARY REWARD

Sometimes the primary rewards are the leaders themselves—or the principles or values they represent. Some people will follow leaders because they embody certain ideals or values, not because they offer pragmatic rewards. This is true in all fields, but especially so in politics. Integrity, trust, dependability should be viewed as significant rewards. When people continue to vote for an incumbent because she or he stands for principles those voters admire, then those principles become the reward.

Good leadership, then, is the best possible reward a leader can give to a follower. Nothing else can take its place. Good leadership is often perceived by followers as a combination of certain qualities. You will discover many of these by completing the exercise on the following page.

A Checklist of Leadership Qualities

Different people look for different qualities in their leaders. Which qualities would you find most satisfying? You can get some indication by completing this exercise. Simply write the number 1 by the quality that represents your first choice, and so on, until you have written the number 10 next to the quality that is least important to you. The rewards (leadership qualities) that please you are probably not very different from the rewards that will please your followers.

I WOULD LIKE A LEADER WHO …

_____ is honest and trustworthy.

_____ is decisive, not wishy-washy.

_____ has the ability to communicate in a clear, forceful manner.

_____ has the strength of character to protect principles important to me.

_____ provides special rewards that are important to me as an individual.

_____ is flexible, who is willing to change when best for followers.

_____ cannot be intimidated by others.

_____ has statesmanlike qualities; that is, someone who thinks of the long-term good and does not get involved in petty issues.

_____ has compassion for others.

_____ is consistent in actions, reliable.

**LEADERS ACCEPT
THE CHALLENGE
OF CREATING
SUPERIOR REWARD
SYSTEMS**

Making MRT work is not easy. It must be accepted as a major challenge. Leaders must provide motivating rewards. They must take into consideration that different followers may want different rewards, and the more followers they have, the more complex the problem becomes.

To discover the right rewards, leaders must be outstanding listeners, sensitive to both the needs of the organization and to the individuals in that organization. They must be able to send rewards to the right target areas at the right time. And then, because they cannot provide all the rewards followers desire, they must decide which rewards make the most sense in view of the situation. It is never a matter of providing all the rewards followers would like, but of providing the best rewards under the circumstances.

Dorothy Dart, the owner of a small electronics firm, called a meeting of her 17 employees to discuss the rewards she was in a position to provide. She clearly stated that she could provide only one of the two rewards in each of the following categories:

- Higher salaries *or* more fringe benefits.

- She could spend more time with her employees in the plant, *or* she could spend more time developing orders in the field.

- Better working conditions now (costly improvements) *or* a new, far superior shop in the future.

Through open and prolonged discussion, with everyone having a voice, the decision was made to provide more benefits instead of a salary increase, more orders from the field instead of more personal attention, and a new shop in the future instead of improvements now. Once the meeting was over, Ms. Dart knew which rewards to provide. With good follow-through, she can now employ MRT to strengthen her organization and her leadership.

**ALL LEADERS MUST
DEVELOP THEIR
OWN REWARD
MATRIX**

A leader of a sizable organization who can see that (1) the right personal rewards are provided to his or her immediate staff members, that (2) all other personnel receive adequate personal rewards from their superiors, and that (3) the right general rewards are provided to everyone in the organization is going to have a strong, cohesive, winning organization. The organization will produce more, and everyone will come out ahead. To accomplish this goal, all leaders must develop their own reward matrix according to the goals of the organization and the needs of its members. This, of course, is the crux of the matter. It is one thing to work out an individual mutual reward exchange where both people come out ahead; it is a far greater challenge to work out a group reward exchange where everybody comes out ahead. MRT does, however, offer this opportunity.

The governor of a state might give personal rewards to his (or her) immediate staff and to the members of both houses of the legislature. He must also give general rewards to the voters in the state. The president of a college might concentrate on personal rewards for his (or her) immediate staff, faculty members, and key administrators. General rewards would be provided to students, alumni, and members of the community.

The President of the United States needs to provide his White House staff with the right personal rewards. Such rewards could be anything from the opportunity to be a privileged insider, to personal recognition for a job well done, to backup support when mistakes are made. In return the President wants complete loyalty, high productivity, and prudent behavior from his staff. The President must also provide general rewards to every citizen (follower) in the country. These, too, must be the right rewards if he wants to be elected again. Primary rewards might be a stronger economy, a more equitable welfare system, or a cleaner environment. *But it must be the right mix of the right rewards at the right time.*

President Eisenhower gave voters some of the key rewards they wanted in the early and mid-fifties. His reputation as a military leader, his midwestern brand of conservatism, his undeniable patriotism appealed to an electorate worried about the Korean war and the threat of international communism.

Some political observers believe that President Carter, as another example, may have miscalculated the rewards voters wanted when he placed so much emphasis on world peace at the expense of domestic matters. Many people, perhaps more than he and his staff recognized, wanted the reward of a stronger economy and safer cities.

Most followers realize that they are not going to get all the rewards they want, but they want those with high priority to receive first attention. The choice of which rewards to provide (and the relative success at providing them) has a great deal to do with the final ratings Presidents receive in history books.

Followers always determine the destiny of their leaders.

PERSONAL VERSUS GENERAL REWARDS

Personal rewards are rewards a leader gives to either a single follower or a small group of followers. Examples are one-on-one conversations, special attention, and individualized forms of recognition. All leaders can and should provide personal rewards to their immediate staff.

What about leaders who must deal with hundreds, thousands, or millions of followers?

Here the leader must also provide general rewards. A general reward is almost always bestowed impersonally (for example, in a company memo or an announcement from the dean's office). Needless to say, a general reward must be designed to please the majority of followers. Some obvious examples of general rewards are tax cuts (government), holidays (school administrations), Christmas bonuses (business), and cost-of-living increases (labor).

It is therefore important that top leaders make sure that their subordinates offer personal rewards to those they lead so that everyone in the group receives both personal and general rewards. General rewards, as welcome as they may be, will not replace the need for personal rewards from the immediate leader.

COMMUNICATION AND GENERAL REWARDS

The larger the organization, the more critical is the need for a good delivery network to make certain that rewards reach their destination. In this respect, MRT is dependent upon the quality of the communication systems within the organization. But MRT, if practiced with vigor and sensitivity, can also make a contribution to improving the communication skills of both leaders and followers. Why?

- Making MRT work forces a leader to become a better listener. You simply cannot provide the right rewards until you know what people want. You find these rewards only when you search and listen.

- Setting up a reward system with a single individual forces both parties to get together to exchange views, negotiate, and learn more about each other.

- People who must depend upon the media to receive rewards from their leaders listen more and respond better when the leader talks about rewards that are important to them—rewards that are uncovered as a result of research and listening.

The number-one side benefit of MRT is better communication. Leaders should practice it for this alone.

Leaders convert nonfollowers into followers through the way they employ MRT in specific situations. They fail as leaders when they forget to do so. Read the cases on page 50. They illustrate what happens when leaders incorporate—or fail to incorporate—MRT into their style.

PRACTICAL APPLICATIONS OF MRT

If MRT is to work, leaders must also receive rewards. In one sense, leaders should not expect as many rewards as followers because there are certain rewards that are automatically built into leadership positions. For example, a psychic payoff takes place the moment one becomes a leader. Some of it comes from follower recognition, but most of it stems from the exercise of power. Most top-level leaders function in an intoxicating environment.

WHAT REWARDS DO LEADERS RECEIVE?

Although highly rewarding, power can be dangerous. Here is a comment from the owner of a manufacturing concern.

> "The heady wine of leadership can send anyone on a disaster trip. The higher the position, the stronger the wine. Beginning leaders must learn to sit on their egos by reminding themselves that leaders are just normal human beings who are supposed to serve their followers and not their own egos. It is not an easy lesson to learn, and as leaders move into more rarified atmospheres, they must learn it over and over again. The problem is one of balance. Leaders must have strong egos to lead; they must also keep thinking well of themselves so they can maintain their personal confidence and continue to lead. But they must eventually learn to live comfortably with the power that is theirs, or their followers will either hope for a fall or actually create it."

Because of the built-in rewards in leadership, leaders should recognize that they will probably give more rewards than they will receive. Leaders should keep in mind that it is sometimes awkward for their subordinates to reward them with more than loyalty and performance. For example, members of the group may want to give their leaders compliments, but because of peer pressure and lack of opportunity, they do not get around to doing so. Leaders who think that their followers are not appreciative

Your Leadership Is Showing

The Presence of Leadership

Slime, the leader of a highly successful punk rock group for over five years, provided the following rewards to the other four members: good musical arrangements, good bookings, and ample opportunities for individual recognition. In return, his musicians were dependable, made maximum use of their talent, and supported him as their leader in all crucial tests. Slime demonstrated his leadership by insisting that the reward system in operation be discussed openly so that everyone understood the trade-off involved. When Slime quit to attend graduate school, the new leader lasted only three months.

Marty discovered quickly that if her fashion boutique were to survive she would not be able to pay more than minimum wages to her part-time staff. How could she compensate? She came up with a reward system that doubled her employees' performance. Marty took each employee on a buying trip, took each out for lunch and lots of fashion conversation once a month, and gave each more opportunities to learn about the business. In doing this, she openly discussed how she could provide some rewards and not others. She demonstrated her leadership ability by saying that the best reward she could provide would be to prepare her employees for higher-paying, more demanding fashion jobs elsewhere.

The Absence of Leadership

Joyce was the personnel director for a large branch of a successful retail chain. She reported directly to the corporate personnel officer. Over a period of three years, Joyce did more than her part in providing all possible rewards to her superior. She researched and introduced some cost-effective procedures; she cut down on personnel turnover; and, most important of all, she solved all these problems without going to the corporate office for help. But Joyce received little recognition from the corporate officer— the one reward she wanted most. As a result, Joyce moved to a competitive company.

Drew was more than upset when he lost his job as a restaurant manager. After all, he had majored in restaurant management in college and had devoted seven years of his life to working his way up to manager. Bob Henry, the vice-president, fired Drew because of low morale, low productivity, and excessive customer complaints. Investigation showed that Drew had not provided a good reward system for his employees. His attitude was that if employees did well, he would reward them with a promotion. He demonstrated his lack of leadership by not discovering and providing daily as well as long-term rewards.

should remember two things: If followers had the opportunity, they would probably provide more personal rewards; if they didn't appreciate the leader, they probably would not be following.

None of this is to say that the leader-follower relationship should not be mutually rewarding. It should. It simply states that there is not perfect parity in the mutual reward system.

Many definitions of leadership state that a true leader is one who can motivate others. L. L. Bernard gave us this definition in 1926: "Any person who is more than ordinarily efficient in carrying psychological stimuli to others and is thus effective in conditioning collective responses may be called a leader."

Bernard's definition is a simple restatement of what the Mutual Reward Theory is all about. When followers receive the appropriate stimuli (rewards), they in turn reward the leader with a positive response. The process can continue indefinitely. The positive responses of the followers elicit more positive stimuli, which in turn create more positive responses. Everyone comes out ahead.

MRT MOTIVATES BOTH PARTIES

Followers make leaders when they agree to follow. Followers break leaders when they change their minds. Followers, and followers alone, provide the franchise to lead. Organizations may appoint leaders, but the ultimate source of power comes from followers. Leadership is therefore the ability to attract and keep followers. Unfortunately, all it takes is a few hostile nonfollowers to undermine the power of a leader. That is why leaders must constantly maintain surveillance. When trouble starts, they need to move in quickly and discover the rewards that will get everyone following again. MRT counseling is an excellent technique to use in these situations. (See the Appendix, pages 145–47.)

THE ULTIMATE FRANCHISE TO LEAD COMES FROM FOLLOWERS

Ultimately, the Mutual Reward Theory will not work if it is used to strengthen the leader's position at the expense of the followers. Followers soon discover when a leader is self-serving. If rewards, both personal and general, do not have a true ring of sincerity, they will not be accepted. If MRT is used simply to manipulate followers, it will surely fail.

As one leader commented, "You might be able to manage without a heart, but you cannot lead effectively without one."

MRT MUST BE FAIR

Leadership Comparison Exercise—MRT

Please reread pages 34–35 for a quick review of the introduction to this exercise. Then rate your three models according to their sensitivity to the needs of their followers. Use the chapter as your guide. Rate on this foundation only; do not be influenced by your previous rating. If you are not personally close to this leader, some guessing may be involved. Your interpretation of your models as kind, tactful, and fair leaders will suffice. Please ask yourself these questions.

- Does this leader demonstrate compassion for others?

- Does she or he have integrity?

- Is this leader sensitive to the needs of others?

- If you are not already a member of this leader's personal staff, would you like to be?

- Once exposed to MRT, would this model quickly accept, adopt, and implement the theory?

- Does this leader, as far as you can tell, have the full backing of his or her immediate staff?

	Strong Points	*Weak Points*
Number 1 _____ (*best at MRT*)	_____ _____ _____ _____	_____ _____ _____ _____
Number 2 _____	_____ _____ _____ _____	_____ _____ _____ _____
Number 3 _____	_____ _____ _____ _____	_____ _____ _____ _____

- The Mutual Reward Theory is the human-relations foundation for the Leadership Formula.

- MRT will give any leadership style more substance.

- Leaders must constantly monitor, and improve, their reward matrix.

- It is not only providing the right number of rewards that makes a good leader, it is providing the right rewards.

- Both personal and general rewards must be provided; the further away the leader is from his or her followers, the more important general rewards become.

- The best reward a leader can provide a follower is good leadership; the best reward a follower can provide a leader is support.

- The more valuable a reward, the fewer are required.

- A good way for a leader to restore a relationship with a follower is to discover a better reward system through MRT counseling.

- The better the reward system works, the more motivated each party becomes.

- MRT should not be used to manipulate followers in an unfair way.

SUMMARY

Applying MRT

Note: Read the MRT cases in the Appendix before you do this exercise.

This exercise is designed to help you prove to yourself that MRT works. You will need to enlist the services of another person or a small group of people. If you can work with a small group—your immediate staff or three or four fellow students—this is recommended. If you decide to work with an individual, select someone with whom you have only a partial or ineffective reward system.

Using the 5 R's of communication, explain the Mutual Reward Theory in your own words. When you have finished, ask the individual or group to indicate the rewards they would like to receive—rewards you are in a position to provide. List these either on a blackboard or on a sheet of paper as illustrated below.

Rewards Desired by Followers	*Rewards Desired by Leader*
1.	1.
2.	2.
3.	3.
4.	4.
5.	5.
6.	6.

The idea is to get all possible rewards from both sides out into the open. In a small group situation, this could take 10 to 20 minutes. With an individual, it may take only a few minutes. It is important, however, to take all the time necessary to uncover the real rewards followers want. Once the followers have expressed their desires, the leader should not hesitate to list those rewards he or she would like. Some give-and-take is usually necessary, but once a list is agreed upon a reward system has been established; if agreeable, both parties can make an informal contract to do their best to live up to the possibilities.

Ralph and Randy are discussing the Mutual Reward Theory on the way home from a religious conference. The theory was introduced by one of the speakers. Ralph is Randy's minister; Randy is an elder.

"Randy," said Ralph, "I'm of the opinion that most good leaders, especially Christians, automatically practice the Mutual Reward Theory."

"I'm not so sure," replied Randy. "In our church, I feel we provide too few rewards to our members and not always the right ones. We lose many members needlessly. For example, the Richardson family left us, and we don't even know why. They were big contributors, too."

"Are you saying that if I and the other leaders of the church would apply the theory that we would serve God better?"

"Yes, I believe that would be true."

"It is too contrived," stated Ralph. "I believe all we need do is demonstrate compassion. When we do this, the rewards are obvious. We don't have to list them."

Randy replied: "I agree that the theory won't work without compassion, but I don't believe compassion will do it alone. We can't build a good reward system without knowing what our congregation wants. We need a more realistic approach if everybody is to come out ahead. For example, I believe it would greatly improve our personal relationship if we could sit down and talk about the rewards we both seek. In a sense you are the leader, and I am the follower. What rewards should I provide? What should I expect from you in return?"

"Perhaps you are right. It might make me a better leader. I'm not so sure, however, that it will be easy for me to do."

Would you recommend that Ralph make a major attempt to weave MRT into his approach as a minister? Because of his compassion for people would it be easier for him? Would he be more successful? What are the chances, in your opinion, that he will make the behavioral changes necessary? (The author's opinion is in the back of the book.)

Case 7: Compassion

Case 8: Fear

Tom Castelletti is the manager of a trucking depot for a large firm. He supervises about 60 truckers and 16 maintenance people. A high-school dropout, he has earned his role as a manager the hard way, starting out as a trucker himself. Bill Nelson, the owner and a strong supporter of Tom, wants him to blend the Mutual Reward Theory into his rough but effective style. He feels it will improve productivity and create a better relationship with the union. Tom is reluctant to make the move for the following reasons. "The moment I start talking about rewards around here they'll want the sky. The first thing will be more money. Then better hours. It will open up a whole can of worms. The idea may be okay in some places, but not around here. We deal in a more basic way with people. They need more discipline, not less. They would just laugh at this approach."

Bill replies. "Tom, I don't think you get the point. There's nothing to be afraid of. Everyone needs certain rewards from their jobs. Some of these rewards you can provide with little effort if you take the trouble to find out what they are. Others may be beyond your power to provide, and you should just say so. All you are doing now is putting out fires. By working out reward systems with your key people and finding out what the truckers really want, you'll be able to do a much better job with less effort. You'll discover when you open up the subject on a person-to-person basis that the individual will ask for fewer rewards than you suspect. What it boils down to is a kind of relationship contract. If you'll produce for me, I'll do my best to provide the rewards you want. It's a very practical approach."

Bill continues. "I'll tell you what I am willing to do. Let's you and I sit down and work out a better reward system between ourselves. You tell me what rewards you want, and I'll do the same. If it works for us, will you be willing to try it on your truckers?"

Will Bill's approach work? Or are Tom's fears justified? Can MRT work in all environments? (See the back of the book for the author's response.)

Mark each statement below True or False.   **Self-Test**

_____   1. MRT will add more substance to any style.

_____   2. You always know when MRT is working because both parties come out ahead.

_____   3. A single high-level reward can sometimes equal or replace many smaller rewards.

_____   4. Generally speaking, leaders provide all the rewards followers need.

_____   5. Anyone who can make MRT work on a day-to-day basis will substantially improve his or her communication skills.

_____   6. The ultimate franchise to lead comes from the organization.

_____   7. MRT is the human-relations foundation of the Leadership Formula; if one ignores it the other foundations are rendered less effective.

_____   8. Providing the right rewards is often more important than providing a great number of rewards.

_____   9. MRT is easy to apply.

_____   10. The best general reward a leader can provide is to be a good leader.

Turn to the back of the book to check your answers.

TOTAL CORRECT _____

Chapter 5

Handle Power with Care

The great principle of all is that no one of either sex should be without a commander.

Plato, Laws XII

OBJECTIVES

After finishing this chapter, you will be able to:

• Determine where your authority line should be.

• Demonstrate stronger leadership through the maintenance of your authority line.

• Make more effective use of your primary sources of power.

The Mutual Reward Theory is an expression of the human-relations side of leadership—the soft side. Structure and discipline are parameters of the other side of leadership—the hard side. The two sides work together. MRT increases the group's tolerance for organizational structure; structure provides the discipline necessary to get the job done. Both are equally important. In fact, one is totally ineffective without the other.

The key to leadership is finding the blend that will work. It is a tightrope every leader must walk daily, as the following example illustrates.

The success of Ruth Reynolds' business college is the talk of the town. Mrs. Reynolds started her school in a dilapidated downtown location seven years ago. Two months ago, the college moved into new modern facilities to handle a student body which has increased 30 percent a year for three successive years. Why has Mrs. Reynolds been so successful? Perhaps because of her well-balanced blend of personal concern for staff and students and her discipline.

Mrs. Reynolds devotes a great deal of time to MRT counseling—with both staff and students. One of her most common questions is, "What can I do for you that I am not doing already?" But there is never any doubt about who is in charge. She sets a work tempo that others emulate. And if someone does not live up to standards, she intervenes quickly and talks openly about it.

One faculty member made this statement: "She has that rare combination of personal touch and powerful leadership. I never feel neglected or unrewarded, but I also know I must live up to my potential. She can be tough when it's required."

Authority, structure, and discipline are the framework of any successful group or organization. They are the tools of control. They prevent disorganization and chaos.

Without such a framework, there will be squabbles, dissension, and confusion. Any group, no matter what its members might say, needs leadership. If provided in the right amount and in the right way, most people welcome and respect it.

Although the words "authority," "structure," and "discipline" have a negative connotation for many (because people connect them with a loss of freedom), they should be positive words to the would-be leader. They are the vehicles that will let him express his leadership.

Every leader must, at times, let her or his leadership show. Authority must be communicated. Structure must be imposed. Timing is important, as the two cases below illustrate.

EXPRESSING YOUR LEADERSHIP

Everyone was amazed when Jeff received the appointment. He was sensitive to the needs of others and a gifted strategist, but people thought he was too soft to be a head coach. Jeff said little for the first two days, letting people react and adjust. Then he called a meeting of the entire team—players and assistant coaches. He sat on a table and stared at his audience for ten minutes until everyone settled down and decided to listen. Jeff then said: "Everyone in this room has a choice. You must decide whether to accept my authority or drop off the team today. Things will be different around here effective now. We are going to do whatever it takes to put a winning team together. If you are out on the field in ten minutes, I'll know you are with me." He then turned and walked away.

Jeff had, through very few words, expressed his leadership. He drew a line. From that moment on everyone, including the other coaches, would know who was in charge. Jeff was still the nice guy he had always been; but he was now a leader as well.

Lorna Henderson accepted her new position as superintendent of the nursing home knowing that she was walking into a hornet's nest. She spent her first two days being friendly but efficient. On the third day, she scheduled ten-

minute private talks with each member of her staff. There was a constant stream of people in and out of her office for six hours. In each interview she made a statement similar to this: "You will find me fair, and I will give you all the rewards and personal time possible. I care about your future, but I have standards that you must live up to. If you do not accept them, I will take corrective action. I intend to turn this nursing home around in 60 days. Once this happens, it will be a much better place for you to work. Are there any questions?"

If leaders do not maintain control, the members of the group begin to go in different directions, and the group becomes fragmented instead of cohesive. If disorder continues, anarchy sets in. The purpose of leadership is to get people to work together toward common goals—to accomplish things that can only be achieved through group effort. The effective leader can make a group achieve more than the sum of its members' individual efforts. None of this can happen, however, without structure. All leaders must at one time or another tighten up the reins, take a firm stand, and take corrective action of some kind.

MAINTAINING STRUCTURE

Ralph Stogdill defines leadership as "the initiation and maintenance of structure in expectation and interaction." This definition implies that the leader is responsible for the development of the structure necessary to maximize group performance in the achievement of organizational goals.

But creating structure and maintaining it does not mean to return to old-fashioned autocratic forms of leadership. It does not mean harsh, arbitrary rules that subordinates must adhere to or else. It does not mean paternalistic leadership, where all group members are expected to honor their leaders whether they deserve it or not. If a Theory Y leadership style doesn't produce the results a leader anticipated, it does not mean that he or she should embrace Theory X*. MRT and clear, decisive leadership

---

*Theory X, management by control, states that workers must be directed and controlled in order to achieve high productivity. Theory Y, participatory management, states that workers will achieve greater productivity if they can direct their own efforts through involvement with organizational goals.

Maintaining an Authority Line

Listed below are twelve techniques, strategies, or approaches that leaders frequently use to maintain their authority lines, add structure, and communicate their leadership. Draw a line through those that you feel will do more harm than good.

Ask politely for follower cooperation.

Reprimand violators openly so that everyone gets the message quickly.

Stand tough on previous decisions so everyone knows you mean business.

Communicate strong leadership through image—circulate in a friendly manner but let your bearing indicate that you are in command.

Speak with authority.

Discipline individual violators in private counseling sessions.

Conduct periodic group meetings in which you encourage discussion, but still show you are in charge.

Be extra tough on immediate staff, and then delegate the maintenance of your authority line to them so that you can appear more benevolent to followers.

Stay with the philosophy that the fewer rules the better as long as group goals are met. Fewer rules mean less maintenance.

Use the group reprimand approach—if the shoe fits, let the follower wear it.

Take care of violations immediately—before you magnify them out of proportion and before the behavior in question becomes a habit with the violator.

Communicate your displeasure without words—let your negative countenance convey the message.

will keep the group headed in the right direction regardless of leadership style.

There is no escape from the fact that every leader must walk that tight line between freedom and control. The Boy Scout leader must give the members of his troop the freedom to exercise initiative, but exert enough control so that they do not get out of hand. The teacher cannot help students reach learning goals without discipline and respect. The corporate president must run a tight ship in order to reach established productivity and profit goals. Even the President of the United States must occasionally take time to do some corrective counseling with an errant cabinet or staff member. Authority must be expressed. No leader can avoid understanding structure. It goes with the territory.

UNDERSTANDING THE AUTHORITY-LINE CONCEPT

All leaders establish an authority line, an imaginary psychological demarcation point between acceptable and unacceptable behavior. It says to organization members, "I will go along with this, but I will draw the line when it comes to that." It is a form of communication (perhaps never verbalized) that says, in effect: "You have all the freedom you need to perform effectively and enjoy yourself, but there is a limit. If you pass my authority line, you can expect some form of discipline." An authority line can also be interpreted as a territorial limit that states: "I respect you and your individual rights and will support you enthusiastically, providing you stay within reasonable bounds."

From a group member's point of view, an authority line is something that can be tested: "I will try to get by with as much as possible, even if I step over the line. It won't hurt my progress in the long run." From a leader's point of view, an authority line states: "We have a contract here. I want to provide as much freedom as possible, but I must also maintain control. I am the leader and I must lead. If matters reach a certain point, I will step in. I am willing to provide certain rewards, but my reward from you is a certain standard of behavior." When a subordinate honors a leader's authority line, he is giving that leader a reward: He is accepting his or her leadership.

How and where an authority line is set is a crucial part of anyone's leadership style. It demonstrates how much leadership is present and how sensitive the leader is in employing it.

Is it possible for a leader to draw a line that will be accepted by all group members, provide the structure needed, and help the group reach predetermined goals? If so, must the line be raised or lowered as conditions change?

To answer these questions, let's look at two widely different examples of authority-line violations.

As a manager, for instance, it may not bother you if an employee is occasionally late in returning from lunch—say, 15 minutes once or twice a week. Your personal tolerance level—related to the authority line you establish—can handle this. But if the same person is 20 minutes late three times a week, you may feel that your tolerance threshold has been crossed, that your authority line has been violated, and some form of discipline is in order. You may say to yourself: "This person does not recognize my leadership role or honor my authority line. My authority is being questioned, and it is time to act. *This person is no longer behaving in a manner I can accept.*"

As a result, you initiate a corrective interview. By taking this action, you have accomplished three things. First, you have used your authority (power) to remind everyone that you have standards. Second, you have adjusted your line as far as recent violations are concerned. Third, and most important, you have clearly expressed your leadership. Although the individual disciplined might react in a negative manner, your other employees might say: "I like the way he leads the department. He doesn't let a few people get away with murder. I just don't like a boss that other people can intimidate." Although readjusting a line may upset violators, it provides necessary group structure. The overall response, at least in the long run, is usually positive.

The President of the United States, in his role as head of the government, establishes a kind of authority line with the Soviet Union. He might state, for example, that if a certain geographical frontier is crossed, a specific action will be taken in response. The United States has a national tolerance level, and once it has been breached (the invasion of an ally), some form of action can be anticipated. The setting and maintenance of authority lines—whether between two leaders or between a leader and a group—is a characteristic of leadership.

If a leader does not take the promised action when his authority is violated, he loses credibility. A discipline line should not be set in the first place unless it can be upheld. Inactivity or indecision is always interpreted as an absence of leadership.

KNOWING WHEN AND WHERE TO DRAW THE LINE

YOUR AUTHORITY LINE

**THREE
AUTHORITY-LINE
MODELS**

It may be helpful to study three authority-line models. Picture a hypothetical situation in which a business office is being converted to a new system of processing data. The office manager wants to get high productivity from all workers throughout the changeover period. She is a staunch believer in MRT, but insecure about where to set her authority line. In analyzing the problem she decides to follow one of three models illustrated below.

Absence of Structure

"These are professionals. Give them freedom and they will produce. The less interference the better. The work itself will provide structure. When they realize that I believe in MRT, they will discipline themselves to protect their rewards. If one or two start to take advantage of the temporary chaos caused by the changeover, I will chat with them individually. I want an open, participative group. If I can provide a free atmosphere, the employees will motivate themselves. The less structure—the higher my authority line—the better."

Heavy Structure

"Accuracy is the key to the success of any data-processing operation. You cannot have accuracy without structure and discipline. My employees will appreciate daily maintenance of high standards. It will provide the security they need. As long as they are provided with all the basic rewards, they will accept the structure. I do not want to stifle people, but this operation calls for a low, tight, consistent line. In the end, they will produce more and be happier for it."

Moderate Structure

"This approach sets a firm, consistent authority line, but provides more freedom than the preceding model. The idea is to support MRT with a good deal of decisive leadership. Give each employee freedom to contribute, freedom to relax, but set a strong line, one that is both fair and clear. When it is violated, take immediate corrective action, but be sensitive about it. I want all employees to feel comfortable and motivated, but I also want them to feel my leadership."

When you are in a leadership role, you will set your own authority line to fit your own style and your own situation. Your judgment will prevail. The three models simply define the range for you.

In setting authority lines, various elements need to be considered. Here are a few:

- Age and other personal characteristics of subordinates, including degree of educational sophistication

- The nature of the work to be accomplished

- Safety factors

- The physical working climate

- The environment created by other authority figures, including your own manager

Just where—at what level—an authority line is established also depends upon the style of the leader. A task-oriented leader will probably set a lower line than a people-oriented leader. Above all else, a line must fit within the "comfort zone" of the leader. He or she must be able to live with it gracefully day in and day out without constantly making changes. Consistency is mandatory.

Although *where* a leader decides to set his or her line is primarily a matter of style, *how* the line is enforced and maintained is an expression of leadership. It is not where a line is set that expresses leadership; it is how violations are treated. A leader who sets a high, permissive line but does not permit anyone to take advantage of it expresses leadership more than one who sets a lower line and permits violations.

In 1981, airline traffic controllers, all federal employees, went on strike after President Reagan had stated that he would not tolerate such action. They tested his authority line and wound up losing their jobs. You may or may not approve of the President's action, but you must agree that it gave him an opportunity to demonstrate his leadership to the entire country.

UNDERSTANDING SOURCES OF POWER

A common definition of leadership is "the sensitive use of power to achieve group goals." All leaders have power—some abundantly more than others—but it is the way power is exercised that determines whether or not the leader is successful.

Power provides the opportunity to be a leader, but it doesn't come with a set of instructions for using it wisely. No warranty is provided. Some leaders fail to use the power they possess; others abuse it; only a few learn to use it skillfully. Establishing an authority line and then protecting it is not the only way a leader expresses power. Power manifests itself in communication, delegation of assignments, and especially in decision making. But nothing impresses subordinates more quickly and clearly than a leader who protects his or her authority line with conviction.

To understand how to use power in a sensitive, acceptable, and effective way, it is necessary to know the sources. Until a leader understands where his power is coming from, he cannot know how to use it effectively to make the most of the opportunity to lead.

The three basic sources of leadership power are: *role power* (the power that goes with the position), *personality power* (power generated by the force of the individual), and *expert power* (power that derives from special skills or knowledge).

In the exercise of leadership all sources of power are always present. You cannot rely totally on any single source. But, to gain better follower reaction, it is sometimes best to soft-pedal one source and emphasize another.

A military officer may derive 70 percent of his or her power from the position itself (role power); 20 percent from personality power; 10 percent from expert power. In a combat assignment, the officer's leadership power derives primarily from his rank (role). In a noncombat assignment, his (or her) expertise or personality might substantially affect, positively or negatively, his image as a leader.

In contrast, a minister of a church may derive 50 percent of his power from personality; 30 percent from knowledge; and 20 percent from the role itself.

USING ROLE POWER EFFECTIVELY

In most cases the power attached to a leadership position is more potent than the person who occupies it realizes. For example, the position of President of the United States has awesome power—no matter who occupies it. To a lesser degree, the same is true of corporate and college presidents, police chiefs, and other government officials. Even the first-line supervisor or volunteer leader has more role power than he or she suspects.

Power Analysis

Although all leaders make use of all three power sources as they play out their roles, some positions call for more emphasis on one source than another. What, in your opinion, would be a reasonable percentage breakdown of the power sources in these leadership roles?

	Lab Manager	*Movie Director*	*Girl Scout Leader*
ROLE POWER	20 %	5 50 %	20 %
PERSONALITY POWER	10 %	50 10 %	60 %
KNOWLEDGE POWER	70 %	20 40 %	10 %
	100%	100%	100%

Role power is generally accepted without question. People know it is not easy to be in a position of authority; in fact, they are often sympathetic to those who are. (How often have you heard someone say about the President, "I wouldn't have his job if they paid me a million dollars a year.") People, however, do not react well to leaders who abuse power. They resent the coach, the senator, the boss who takes advantage of the power engendered by his or her position. The coach who bullies his players, the senator who doesn't vote on key issues, the boss who betrays his employees' trust will soon find themselves without followers.

Generally speaking, the best way to use role power is to let it work silently. Live with that power comfortably and use it gracefully. Recognize it, but don't let it go to your head.

Role power, however, is there to be used and should be communicated without hesitation under certain circumstances— for example, when an authority line needs to be lowered. No other source of power will reestablish the leader's authority quicker, as the following examples illustrate.

"Frank, the difference between you and me is that I am sitting in the chair of the president. You don't have to like me as a person, but you must respect my position. From now on I expect you to conform to policy like everyone else."

"Okay, everybody. We made excellent progress last month, but we still need to eliminate some safety violations. Keep in mind that my position forces me to take disciplinary action if necessary. The same would be true if you had my job."

"There is nothing personal about it, but as long as I occupy this position, that's the way it will be. No exceptions."

Some successful leaders stress their role power only as a last resort—when, for example, the well-being of the organization is threatened. In general, good leaders just sit back—slightly aloof—and let role power work for them. They do not overplay or underplay it; they simply let it add strength to their leadership style.

USING PERSONALITY POWER

Every individual—whether in a leadership role or not—has personality power. We can all use our own personalities to influence others. Those who have a positive attitude, a pleasant voice, a decisive manner, and a strong sex identity frequently have the most impact.

Charisma is a word that we hear frequently today. Some leaders have it in abundance; others have none. Movie stars who have it are winners at the box office; politicians who do not have it may find it more difficult to get elected. But what is it?

Webster's *New World Dictionary* defines charisma as "a special quality of leadership that captures the popular imagination and inspires unswerving allegiance and devotion." Charismatic people apparently have a star quality that makes people want to follow them. Charisma is great for those who possess it. If you do not have it, however, it does not mean that you have no personality power.

You do.

Personality power becomes important in positions of leadership that are inherently weak in role power. For example, many teachers recognize that their role as classroom leader does not have high power content, so they tap their personality power more heavily. They do not say, "Look, I'm the teacher so what I

Leadership and Charisma

Rate the following Presidents (on a scale of one through ten) on their leadership ability and charisma.

Leadership		*Charisma*
7	Harry Truman	7
10	Dwight Eisenhower	8
8	John Kennedy	10 ☆
5	Lyndon Johnson	6
4	Richard Nixon	6
7	Gerald Ford	5 ☆
5	Jimmy Carter	4

Study your ratings. Is there any correlation—either positive or negative—between leadership and charisma? What conclusions can you draw about the role charisma plays in the development of leadership qualities?

---

say goes." Rather they skillfully employ their personality power to achieve higher learning levels. This is true of many leadership roles—volunteer leaders, ministers, elected leaders in trade, fraternal, and social organizations. They get more voltage from the power of their personalities than from the roles they occupy.

The 1980 National Democratic Convention provided an excellent contrast in the use of role versus personality power. President Carter leaned heavily on his role as President and head of the Democratic Party, whereas Senator Kennedy leaned heavily on his personality power. The leadership profiles communicated were different because the power sources were different.

When a "power personality" occupies a "power role," you always have the possibility of outstanding leadership, provided that both power sources are used effectively.

MAKING THE MOST OF EXPERT POWER

When a leader has special skills and knowledge to back up the leadership role he or she occupies, an additional source of power is generated. This is *expert power*. People like to be led by those who know the answers. They look up to those with expertise, giving them more authority than they would otherwise possess. Knowledge—real or imagined—is power.

Being recognized as an expert gives you additional clout. For example, a major who went to West Point is generally more respected than one who graduated from Officers Candidate School. A president of a genetic engineering company who has a Ph.D. in biochemistry is listened to more closely than one who studied business. True expertise, then, generates power automatically.

Sometimes, expert power can be more important than any other kind. For example, the pilot of an airliner is the captain (role power); he may have a strong personal presence (personality power); but it is his ability to fly the plane safely that is the source of his primary power. In a rough sky, skill is what counts—not the title he carries or the charm he may possess.

Leadership itself is expertise.

Many times leadership skills are valued more highly than technical competence. In fact, in most high-level leadership roles, one is more likely to find people with leadership skills than technical competence. The best engineer in the world cannot run an engineering firm without leadership ability. The winning combination, of course, is leadership capabilities and technical knowledge.

The primary danger for those who possess expertise is relying on it too heavily. The know-it-all leader soon loses both friends and followers. The leader who refuses to listen is quickly in trouble. But the leader who has both technical expertise and leadership ability has a definite edge. Sometimes knowledge can be the primary source of power as this case illustrates.

Brenda majored in mathematics and minored in computer science in college. It turned out to be a perfect combination because she was hired by a computer manufacturer the day after graduation. In less than two years, Brenda was offered a job with a client organization. They (the board of the client company) wanted someone to manage those who were going to operate the computer equipment they had bought from Brenda's firm. She took the job, at a big jump in pay and a drop in status. She was given the title of acting manager, which diminished her role power. On top of this, Brenda was a rather quiet, unassuming, work-oriented person. She would be the first to admit that she had little personality power. So Brenda relied heavily—almost 90 percent—on her knowledge of what she was doing.

It didn't take long for those in her department to sense how lucky they were to have her as an acting manager. She seemed to be able to come up with the solution to any computer or programming problem. In addition, she was a great teacher. She always took time to explain how things operated and why it was wiser to do something one way than another. Because of her knowledge (and her ability to communicate it), Brenda earned the respect of her subordinates without having a great deal of role or personality power.

It wasn't long before Brenda was appointed manager of the computer center (no longer acting), and after a while she became more confident because of the positive feedback she received from the people in her department. But even after she gained more role and personality power, she was respected (and followed) primarily because of her knowledge. She had, for that department at least, the right blend of power for a leadership style.

Technical and scientific experts, as well as other specialists, are often short on personality power. Many a research and development person has been promoted into a leadership role only to request a transfer back to the laboratory or design bench. Many an outstanding salesperson has tried out the role of sales manager only to return to the field. In such cases, it is usually a failure to understand or make use of the elements that make up a power base.

INCREASING YOUR POWER BASE

The best way to use the power inherent in your role is to occupy that position with ease, grace, and confidence. Power goes with the role but your sense of presence either increases or decreases your authority.

You increase your personality power by learning how to capitalize on your strong traits and strengthening your weak ones.

You increase your expert power by learning more about the technology and skills in your special area. The more you know, the more you will be able to communicate to subordinates. The more knowledge you communicate the more respect (and power) they will give you.

In any given situation, all power sources available to the leader are automatically drawn upon. They cannot be clearly separated. The leader, however, can often be more effective if he or she uses one source of power rather than another. To provide some preliminary practice in how different power sources might be emphasized in different situations, the following exercise in power sources has been developed. Please read the situation first, and then select the one or two sources of power you feel would best accomplish the task at hand with as little negative reaction as possible.

Followers study their leaders carefully and are more sensitive to how leaders use power than the leaders themselves realize. Although group members may not respond immediately to their leader's use, or abuse, of power (they may be busy adjusting to a new authority line or working harder to reach a group goal), the image they form of the leader is, in large part, determined by the way he handles power.

This is an important factor when you consider that the ultimate source of a leader's power is the people he leads.

What Power Source Would You Use?

Situation	Role Power	Personality Power	Expert Power
1. Insubordination by an employee in a nuclear power plant.	☑	☐	☐
2. Retraining an older employee to operate a new-generation computer.	☐	☐	☐
3. Motivating a staff employee whose productivity has dropped dramatically.	☐	☐	☐
4. Lowering the authority line on all subordinates because of infractions by a few.	☐	☐	☐
5. President of United States giving a State of the Union address to Congress (and the country via television).	☐	☐	☐
6. Minister appearing before congregation to ask for financial pledges.	☐	☐	☐
7. Manager using MRT to counsel a valued employee who has been acting hostile recently.	☐	☐	☐
8. Announcing the discovery of a theft ring and a plan to combat a recurrence in the future.	☑	☐	☐
9. Selling the need for a new piece of technical equipment to your superiors.	☐	☐	☐
10. Announcing a layoff in your organization.	☐	☐	☐
11. College president appearing before faculty for the first time.	☐	☐	☐
12. Police chief speaking before graduating class of police academy.	☐	☐	☐

Leadership Comparison Exercise—Power

In this exercise, you are to rate your three models on the way they deal with structure in their respective organizations or group. The material in the chapter is your guide. Please ask yourself these questions.

- Does the leader provide enough structure to create a cohesive feeling among members of the group?

- Does she or he provide the right balance between authority and individual needs so that everyone wins?

- Is your leader's authority line clear, consistent, and at the right level for the environment?

- Is the authority line maintained with fairness, vigor, and decisiveness?

- Do group members respect his or her authority line?

- Does this leader show sensitivity in the use of role, personality, and knowledge power?

- Is this leader measurably weak in the use of one or more sources of power?

Proceed to rate each of your three models without any reference to previous ratings on other foundations.

	Strong Points	*Weak Points*
Number 1 _____ (*best at using power*)	_____ _____ _____	_____ _____ _____
Number 2 _____	_____ _____ _____	_____ _____ _____
Number 3 _____	_____ _____ _____	_____ _____ _____

- The sensitive application of MRT makes the addition of more structure more acceptable.

- When the chips are down, most people prefer strong, firm leaders.

- Where you set your authority line is important; the way you maintain it is critical.

- You can have a quiet, sensitive, low-key leadership style and still establish and protect a firm authority line.

- Let the power of your role do as much talking for you as possible.

- Develop and use your personality power with sensitivity, but use it.

- Expand your knowledge; but here again, let it speak for itself.

- If you don't show your leadership, others will not know you have it.

SUMMARY

Authority and Power Survey

This exercise is designed for those who occupy a leadership or management position and feel comfortable in approaching their subordinates with a questionnaire that will evaluate their leadership ability. It is also usable in classes, seminars, and workshops if the instructor is willing to play the role of leader and believes students will benefit from evaluating his or her style.

Instructions: Photocopy the questionnaire on the following page, and pass out one copy to each subordinate (or student). Have him or her complete the questionnaire and turn it in to a person who has been designated to prepare a summary sheet. (This procedure protects the respondents' anonymity.) Share the results with everyone.

You may wish to take a few minutes to go over the questionnaire and explain the questions in more detail so that the answers will be more objective.

The more the answers are discussed openly between leader and subordinates, the more everyone will learn.

Authority and Power Questionnaire

Your leader, manager, or teacher wants to know how skill-fully he or she uses authority and power. As a group member, employee, or student you are in a position to communicate, through this questionnaire, just how effectively he or she is operating. Please answer the following questions to the best of your ability.

1. An authority line is defined as that point beyond which a subordinate should not trespass. Do you feel this line is too tight (too little freedom), too loose (too much freedom), or just right?

    Too tight ☐   Too loose ☐   Just right ☐

2. Once your manager sets an authority line does she (or he) maintain it consistently or does she tend to waver?

    Consistent ☐   Wavers ☐

3. A leader has three sources of power. The first is role power that goes with the position; the second is personality power that comes from the individual as a special person; and the third is expert power—the knowledge the leader brings to the position. Check which source of power your manager should rely on more.

    Role power ☐   Personality power ☐   Expert power ☐

4. Check which source of power your leader should stress less.

    Role power ☐   Personality power ☐   Expert power ☐

5. Name three things that your leader could do to make you a more enthusiastic follower.

    _____

    _____

    _____

Case 9: Courage

Jane and Gloria are unlikely friends. Jane is a small, quiet, timid woman of 36 whose marriage has recently fallen apart. She has returned to college in an effort to find a career that will help her put her life back together. Gloria is a powerful personality who operates a successful health spa. They met when Jane joined Gloria's spa.

One evening, after closing the club, Jane and Gloria stopped in a nearby coffee shop. Jane began to talk about Gloria's behavior in class that night.

"Gloria, I'm amazed at how you can stand up for yourself when somebody starts to get out of line. Like tonight, you really put that John Spencer in his place. How can you do this?"

"In my opinion, leadership is 90 percent guts. Every once in a while, I actually look for an opportunity to get tough. Afterward, things go better."

"Wish I were more like you. Frankly, I'll never be a leader—I just don't have the courage. I've been a follower all my life, so I guess I'll stay one."

"Anybody can be a leader if they really want to. I'm looking for an assistant right now. If you let me train you, you can have the job. I can give you the confidence you need to step out and run things when I'm gone."

Do you believe Gloria can convert Jane into a leader? Or are some people born to be followers? Defend your position. (And then turn to the back of the book to discover the author's position.)

Major Brokaw and Captain Small are attending the same military leadership seminar. Major Brokaw has almost thirty years of service. Captain Small has less than ten. They are discussing the problem of blending the Mutual Reward Theory and additional structure together.

"So far I'm not impressed with the formula proposed by our instructor. I understand MRT, but I think it is a weak approach. If I start out with such a soft human-relations approach and then suddenly add more discipline, I'll be in trouble. It's like trying to mix oil and water. I believe the rewards one can get in the military are self-evident. Can you imagine me sitting down with a corporal and asking what rewards he expects from me?"

"Yes, I can," replied Captain Small. "I think it would be a good investment of your time. You'd discover what rewards are required these days to build motivation. And I think you would learn a great deal about yourself."

"Okay. I might give it a try. But I still can't see how MRT and more structure go together. To me, they are just not compatible."

"On the contrary. In my opinion, the more you use MRT, the more structure your men will accept. You see, you start out on a human basis, and once your men know that you will give them certain rewards, then they will accept discipline more readily. It's the combination that works. When you use MRT first, you set the stage for more structure, not the other way around."

Captain Small continues. "We sure see things differently. I don't think of MRT as a weak approach. Just good sense. As a leader, I have a contract with the men under my command. The better the contract the better the relationship, and the better the relationship, the more I can expect from them under stress. I want them to accept my orders when they are necessary. That's why I use MRT."

Do you agree or disagree with Captain Small? Are MRT and structure more compatible in some environments than others? Should the military experiment with the formula? Do you agree that those leaders who do a good job with MRT will be able to apply more structure without getting resistance? Is it possible to be a compassionate leader in the modern military establishment? (Read the author's reaction in the back of the book.)

Case 10: Compatibility

Self-Test Mark each statement below True or False.

_____ 1. The more MRT is used, the more structure subordinates will accept.

_____ 2. Structure without MRT can be counterproductive.

_____ 3. Role power is personality based.

_____ 4. An authority line is an imaginary, psychological point beyond which a subordinate knows he or she should not trespass.

_____ 5. Scientists make excellent leaders because they have more expert power.

_____ 6. Overemphasis on one source of power while neglecting others can injure the leader's image.

_____ 7. Charisma is part of personality power.

_____ 8. All successful leaders have charisma.

_____ 9. It is impossible for a beginning manager to expand his or her power base.

_____ 10. One of the best ways to demonstrate more leadership is to provide more structure.

Turn to the back of the book to check your answers.

TOTAL CORRECT _____

Chapter 6

Learn to Make Decisions with Confidence

Not to decide is to decide.

Harvey Cox

OBJECTIVES

After finishing this chapter, you will be able to:

• Make better decisions.

• Make them faster.

• Announce them with more decisiveness.

A chartered plane flying over dense jungle crashes. Both pilots are killed. The 40 passengers, unharmed but in shock, sit around wondering how to get back to civilization. None of the passengers has had jungle survival training. Through the group process, they decide that their chances of survival will be greater if they stick together and choose a single, strong leader.

What kind of a person should they choose?

Many factors come to mind, but far and above the most important personal quality is the ability to make good decisions. Which direction should the party take? What about food and water? Shelter from the elements? Protection from jungle insects? The moment a leader is chosen, he or she must make decisions quickly and with authority.

In any and all leader-follower situations good decision making eventually surfaces as a characteristic followers value highly. Leaders say the same thing in many ways.

"Poor decision making is the downfall of most leaders."

"Decision making is a symbol of leadership."

"It's not just making good decisions, it's making them with authority and decisiveness."

"Every decision I make has something to do with the health of my corporation. It's when I make these decisions that I know I'm the leader."

"Making decisions is the most demanding thing I do."

"I get paid plenty for being a leader, but it's only when I make a hard decision that I know I have earned it."

"I'm accepted as the leader of this organization because I have been able to take it in the right direction. They may not vote for me on a popularity basis, but they respect me as a decision maker. That is why I remain their leader."

The rank and file also agree that decision making should be an integral part of the Leadership Formula.

"We are totally dependent on the quality of decisions made at the top. If they are bad, we all get hurt."

"It is certainly easy to follow a leader with charisma, but if he doesn't make the right decisions, my job is on the line."

"You quickly lose respect for a leader who can't make good decisions."

"There is nothing more frustrating than having to work for someone who can't make up his mind."

Reaction

Take a moment to react to the following statements. Then, after you have marked each statement true or false, write a single sentence to justify your choice.

_____   A poor decision is better than no decision at all.

_____

_____

_____

_____   Gut, or intuitive, decisions should be avoided at all costs.

_____

_____

_____

_____   In making decisions, most leaders are self-serving; that is, they put their own future ahead of the welfare of the organization and its members.

_____

_____

_____

MAKING GOOD DECISIONS INCREASES YOUR SUPPORT

When a coach makes superior decisions, players win games and feel good about their leadership. When a mayor makes good decisions, the quality of life in the city improves. When a corporate president makes the right decisions, everyone who works for the company benefits.

There is a classic example of the importance of good decision making from the world of business. After World War II, Montgomery Ward, under the leadership of Sewell Avery, decided to retrench and conserve capital until after a predicted recession had passed. Sears Roebuck, on the other hand, decided to expand, sensing that a boom period was around the corner. As a result, Sears became the number-one retailer in the world while Wards lost ground. Everyone connected with Sears developed the feeling of pride that comes from playing on a winning team. Good decisions had earned their support.

Everyone can and should contribute, where possible, to the decision-making process. In the final analysis, however, leaders make the critical decisions. The burden is theirs.

Our dependence on the decision-making ability of our leaders cannot be overestimated. For example, President Harry Truman was forced into making some tough decisions while in office. We are still living with the atomic bomb decision. The destiny of any group, organization, or country lies with the decisions made by its leader. There is no escape.

DEVELOPING YOUR OWN DECISION-MAKING PROCESS

If you improve your decision making you will increase your power and add more leadership to your style.

Decision making has never been easy. It never will be. Leaders who can communicate well, use MRT sensitively, and exercise power wisely may ultimately fail because of poor decision making. Even those who are good at it make a few bad decisions that come back to haunt them. No one bats 1000.

How can you improve your average? First, follow these three steps and then develop a process that fits your comfort zone.

1. Sit down in a quiet place alone. Do not make major decisions on the run or under pressure.

2. Clear all distracting elements from your mind. Good decisions require clear concentration.

3. Using a pencil, follow a process similar to the one on the following page.

© 1984 SRA

A Decision-Making Process

The purpose of this model is to show how the decision-making process works. First, read the entries under the column titled "Process." Note that there is one step for each letter in the word "decisions." Next, read the entries under "Instructions" so that you will be able to apply the process to any decision you make in the future. Read carefully, because later you will be asked to use this process to work through a decision you must make.

Process	*Instructions*
Define desired outcome.	You need to know exactly what you want to accomplish before you can decide the best way to do it.
Establish decision criteria.	What are the guideposts? For example, if you were deciding whether to drive or take the bus to work, you would consider factors like wear and tear on car, safety, cost, and time saved.
Come up with alternative solutions.	Write out all possible courses of action that will lead to the desired outcome.
Investigate—get all possible facts.	Accumulate as many facts as time permits. List them on a separate sheet of paper.
Settle on top three choices.	List them.
Instigate a comparison.	Weigh the three choices and decide between them. Consult with others if necessary.
Opt for the best choice.	List your final decision.
Notify those involved with decisiveness.	The way you articulate your decision can be as important as the quality of the decision itself. Write how you intend to announce it.
See that decision is fully implemented.	A good decision must be made to work. Write out how you intend to do this.

THE MORE LOGIC THE BETTER

Do leaders actually follow models like the one illustrated each time they make a decision? Do they always stop, clear their minds, and then proceed, step by step, through a structured procedure? Most do not, but those who rely heavily on some form of logical process make better decisions.

In the first place, few leaders ever find a single procedure that is always reliable. Most experiment with a number of approaches, constantly attempting to improve their skills. Second, decision makers seem to select different procedures (if they use any at all) for different kinds of problems. For example, they might follow a structured pattern for a major problem, a more intuitive pattern for a minor one.

Finally, and perhaps most important, there is not always time for a formal step-by-step analysis of problem situations. As one leader stated,

"Despite all the computer data available to me, I must still make most decisions in my guts. I just don't have time to gather and fully analyze all the facts. Things are moving too fast. There are too many emergencies."

But every leader should, when possible, follow a logical pattern to improve the quality of decisions. Leaders who do reduce the risk of making bad decisions. Our model shows what some experts might consider an ideal process under ideal conditions. You may never find an "ideal condition," but eventually you need to develop a process that works for you. This may be, as most leaders claim, a never-ending search that will always require adjustments and improvements to fit the situation. But the effort must be made.

CLARITY OF THINKING

It stands to reason that clear thinking is required for good decision making. A muddled mind will not make a clear decision. No argument here. For many decision makers, time and place have a great deal to do with clear thinking. Some people claim they think more clearly early in the morning after a good night's sleep and before the daily pressures pile up. Others say that they must get away to another environment to sort things out more clearly. A growing number of executive runners claim that running produces a "clarity of thinking" that can produce better decisions. Each individual needs to experience many different decision-making climates to discover the one that works best.

Obviously, anything a decision maker can do to clear his or her head for thinking is worth doing. If President Reagan makes better decisions while chopping wood at his California ranch, all of us benefit.

Leaders must be careful not to spend so much of their time perfecting their decision-making systems that they cannot provide direction when it is needed. When there is indecision, organizations become fragmented and employees scramble in different directions.

INDECISION IS A BAD DECISION

> Everyone had high hopes for the new university president. He was a disciplined academician, an accomplished writer, a good communicator, and an outstanding manager. But it soon became apparent that he could not make hard decisions quickly. In fact, the backlog of problems requiring major decisions nearly brought the university to a standstill. For example, in a time of increasing enrollments he refused to trim the fat from his administrative staff and hire more teachers, which resulted in heavier teaching loads for his already overburdened teaching staff. This eventually caused a faculty rebellion. When his four-year contract was up, the university was in shambles.

Hudson T. Armerding, President of Wheaton College, made the following statement in his book *Leadership**: "I prefer someone who acts—even if he makes mistakes on occasion. I believe that if he is 51 percent right in his actions, he is performing more satisfactorily than if he does nothing."

Sweeping problems under a rug is abdicating the leadership role. Good or bad, decisions must be made.

Not only should decisions be made within a reasonable length of time, they should be made with decisiveness. A decision, no matter how small it may be, should show the presence of leadership.

Smart leaders capitalize on opportunities to announce decisions they feel good about. You hear them saying something to this effect: "I am proud to make this announcement. This

---

*Published by Tyndale House, Wheaton, Ill., 1978.

decision takes our organization in the right direction. All of us will come out ahead."

In announcing a decision leaders should use their role power to set the stage and gain the attention of followers, their personality power to present the decision in the best possible light, and their expert power to communicate why the decision is a good one based upon the facts.

DECISION MAKING AND IMAGE

Despite the fact that the rank and file may not always appear interested in the decisions their leaders make, there is a high correlation between the ability to make decisions and the image a leader projects.

> Greg made a hard decision when three of his key players were caught using drugs. They were off the team for the season. A tough decision, but the rest of the players, as well as school officials, recognized it as the right one. Although they lost the next few games, the team got into the playoffs. The following year Greg discovered he had more support from players, administrators, and parents than ever before. His image had been enhanced.

> Victoria, who was the city's recreation director, recommended closing the downtown swimming pool when it became obvious that there was not enough money to keep all three city pools open. Besides, she argued, the downtown pool, which was used primarily by poor minorities, was a big source of trouble. Victoria completely underestimated the reaction from the community, and within ten days she had to withdraw her recommendation. As a result of her ill-advised decision, her image was damaged, and she knew it.

When a leader makes a decision that most people will react positively to, he (or she) should see that the message is widely broadcast. It can only enhance his image. On the other hand, if an unpopular decision must be made, it should be soft-pedaled. When a leader makes a bad decision (and discovers it in time), he can only hope that it will not receive too much publicity, assuming, of course, that he has some control over the media. This is not always the case. When leaders in the public sector make serious mistakes, the prying eye of the media will generally uncover them. Sometimes public reaction can destroy a leader.

All leaders wind up making a bad decision now and then, and generally everybody finds out about it. When this happens, it is the way in which they live with that decision that determines their real leadership capabilities. Those who quickly admit they made a mistake and openly attempt to repair the damage usually come out ahead.

LIVING WITH A BAD DECISION

Raymond was dean of student activities for a large university. When he discovered that a few star football players had been given credit for courses they did not attend, he made the decision to keep it to himself, but to make sure the practice was stopped immediately. Later, because of an NCAA investigation, it all came out. Raymond quickly admitted he had made the wrong decision and apologized to the administration and to the student body. He make no further attempts to cover up. Although some damage was done to his image, he survived the total investigation; and, at least in the eyes of a few people, wound up with more stature than he had before.

It is not easy to live with a bad decision. It can destroy personal confidence and cause the decision maker to be more indecisive in the future. Additionally, it can undermine anyone's faith in his or her ability to make good decisions.

Helen knew she had made a mistake the second day after she had appointed Rick her assistant. He did nothing but rub everyone the wrong way. Productivity slumped. As a result, she lost confidence in herself to make good decisions, and things went from bad to worse. When it was all over— and she had resigned—Helen decided she did not want any kind of leadership role in the future. Decision making was not her cup of tea.

A few bad decisions do not a poor leader make. A leader's overall image counts more than his won/loss record. Nobody keeps records anyway. One way to compensate for a bad decision is to quickly make others that neutralize or offset the first one.

When Sam discovered that he had made a serious mistake by recommending that his firm establish a legal clinic in the city of Cypress, he made a series of other decisions to offset his mistake. First, he admitted that his site research had been faulty. Second, he quickly closed the clinic and announced that he had been able to sublet the building to the advantage of the firm. Third, he worked up new procedures for making better site selections in the future. These new decisions helped to compensate for the damage the first decision did to his image. He also showed strong leadership by demonstrating that he could handle mistakes without losing confidence in himself.

DECISION REVERSALS

Decision reversals are common, and they have less impact upon the leader's image than one might expect. Many leaders told me that, in their opinion, they lose far less respect when they openly reverse a bad decision than when they let it simmer. Apparently the rank and file has a higher tolerance for bad decisions than most people suspect, as this quotation implies.

> "I believe most followers view their leaders as they do their favorite baseball players. They do not expect their leaders to bat 1000 on decision making. Not that they don't hold their leaders accountable, they do; but they don't expect the impossible."

Decision making may be a primary criterion for superior leadership, but no one expects miracles. People want decisive decisions; they want quick decisions; and they want decisions that are good for the organization and themselves. And if a bad decision is made, they want their leaders to acknowledge their part in it, and then do something about it before everyone is hurt even more. *A reversal is far more acceptable than a bad decision that is allowed to remain in force.*

DECISION FLIP-FLOPS DESTROY LEADERSHIP

A leader who makes a serious mistake (and then corrects it) is forgiven. But the leader who reverses a decision because of pressure from special-interest groups is respected by no one. It is true that the best decision is the one that benefits everyone concerned, but when it is impossible to please all subgroups, a decision must still be made. Once the best possible decision has been made, it is wise to stick with it even though not everyone is happy. Leaders who permit pressure from one group to cause them to flip-flop on a decision usually wind up making everyone unhappy.

DECISION MAKING AND THE GROUP PROCESS

Progressive organizations have strengthened themselves by taking the time to involve employees in those decisions that affect them the most. Employees gain ego satisfaction from being involved and are more apt to be enthusiastic about decisions they have participated in. Morale improves. There are two situations in which involving subordinates is especially wise. First, when you as a leader need more information. Second, when it is necessary to eliminate resistance to whatever the ultimate decision will be.

But the dangers of rank-and-file involvement sometimes outweigh the advantages. If the process takes too long, the decision may be delayed (and the leader accused of indecisiveness). Another danger is involving some subordinates and not others, creating dissension and divisiveness in the ranks. The biggest danger of all is that the group will come up with a "committee" decision, one so full of compromises that it is less effective than the one the leader could have made alone. Then the leader is involved in a no-win situation. He must either go along with the decision or override it. If he overrides it, the problems that result will probably be much greater than those created by living with it.

Time permitting, democratic decision making can produce outstanding results. In many situations it is the best approach to take. On the other hand, too much consultation communicates leadership weakness. The right balance is hard to achieve.

COURAGE AND DECISION MAKING

Courage and leadership are first cousins. Insecure people who are always looking for ways to protect themselves, or who prefer to stay out of the limelight, do not become good leaders. People who will do anything to keep people liking them do not become effective leaders. People who avoid controversy at all costs do not become long-term leaders.

Courage means taking a stand that is not popular but is best for the group. It means making a tough decision, knowing you

Testing Your Decision-Making Skills

Mr. Cable is the president-owner of a computer-hardware manufacturing firm with over 200 employees. His leadership style is low-key, participatory, and employee-centered. His firm has excellent employee benefits, including a profit-sharing plan. He delegates responsibility when possible. He involves his management team on almost every decision.

Mr. Cable returned home last night from a two-week marketing jaunt to increase lagging sales. No sooner did he get his bags unpacked than he received a call from factory security. The security officer informed him that the local police had arrested two of his employees for selling dope in the parking lot during the 5 o'clock shift change. The security officer told him that recent surveillance produced evidence of considerable drinking on the premises during working hours. They also have evidence of employee ripoffs.

Mr. Cable immediately called his plant foreman to verify that the two arrested were actually employees. They were. His foreman, however, had not heard of the incident.

The news deeply upset Mr. Cable, but he said to himself: "This is decision-making time. Have a cup of coffee and design three possible strategies you can implement in the morning. Then have a good night's sleep." The three solutions Mr. Cable wrote out on a sheet of paper are as follows.

SOLUTION 1. *Delegate*. Call an immediate meeting of the management team. Turn the drinking and rip-off problem over to plant manager. State that you want an immediate report on how widespread the problem is and that you want the entire mess cleaned up within thirty days.

SOLUTION 2. *Direct action—no consultation*. Get tough this time. Prepare a bulletin for distribution to all employees stating that theft and use of drugs or liquor will be cause for immediate dismissal. Show up at all shift changes. Lay down the law at an emergency management meeting. Use the incident to create a general shake-up of the entire organization.

Testing Your Decision Making Skills
(*continued*)

SOLUTION 3. *Delayed action—general involvement.* Through open discussions with the management team and special groups of employees from each shift, assess all aspects of the problem. Discuss your findings with the police to get their recommendations. After all data has been accumulated, and as many people as possible have been involved, have the personnel officer develop a new written policy for general distribution.

Which of the three possible solutions would you choose? What changes would you make to improve your choice? Think carefully (use the margins to make notes), and then compare your answer with that of the author below.

Author's suggested answer: With a few variations, the author supports Solution 2 for these reasons: (1) There is an apparent lack of leadership within the organization. Mr. Cable should fill this gap himself as soon as possible. He has apparently permitted his authority line to drift too high, and employees are taking advantage of the situation. (2) The members of the management team may need to feel a new surge of leadership at the top even more than line employees. The bulletin will convey the message sooner and with more impact. (3) Delaying action for more than a day could do more harm than good. Rumors could hurt productivity. Expensive equipment could be damaged. The image of the firm could be hurt locally. (4) The nature of the problem does not lend itself to group involvement.

The author feels, however, that Mr. Cable might take one full day to gain additional facts before taking action. He might uncover other violations that were not mentioned. He might also discover that security has overstated the problem, and only a few employees are involved. He needs to review his legal position regarding dismissal actions. With more facts, Solution 2 could be improved upon.

might be proved wrong at a later date. It means saying no to someone you like, knowing that he or she may turn against you in the future. It means risking rejection by people you care about because you must make an unpopular decision.

Generally speaking, people who postpone making a difficult decision do so because they lack the courage to make it. Those who form committees and ask for recommendations when they already have the facts are often delaying decisions to get themselves off the hook. All leaders must make some hard decisions, and making them usually takes guts. There is no escape.

EMOTIONAL STRENGTH— A NECESSITY

Leaders recognize that some isolation from their subordinates, even members of their immediate staff, is part of the role they play. (It is indeed often lonely at the top.) This automatically means that leaders must rely heavily on their own inner strengths and resources.

Leaders who have emotional strength stay calm in turmoil. They handle stress without becoming too discouraged. They handle outside criticism without taking it too personally. Only subordinates enjoy the luxury of relaxing under the protective umbrella of the organization. They can, for the most part, pass on stress.

Leaders cannot become part of the crowd. They must take defeat and bounce back. They must live through traumatic reversals. They must accept the fact that leaders are not always popular. They must learn to live with the fact that both their actions and their words will be misinterpreted.

A FINAL WORD

If you are going to put more leadership into your style through better, more decisive decision making, it is a do-it-yourself project. The effort, however, is worth it. Success will earn you greater respect from those who are dependent on your leadership because good decision making is a reward they will appreciate. Good decisions will either keep you in your present leadership role longer—or open the door to a better one.

Leadership Comparison Exercise—Decisions

Please rate your three models separately on their decision-making skills. In doing this, keep in mind that the direction an organization takes (good or bad) is usually determined by its leaders' decisions. In making your analysis, ask yourself these questions.

- Does this leader consult with advisers before making a decision?
- What kind of decision-making track record does he or she have?
- Would you be willing to accept and follow a decision made by this leader even though you were not consulted?
- Does this leader announce the decisions he or she makes with pride and decisiveness?
- Is your model big enough to admit a mistake and change a bad decision?
- Are you satisfied that the leader studies all possible data, uses a logical process, and then, under the circumstances, makes the best possible decision?
- Does he or she face up to hard decisions and make them quickly?

	Strong Points	Weak Points
Number 1 _____ (*best at decisions*)	_____ _____ _____	_____ _____ _____
Number 2 _____	_____ _____ _____	_____ _____ _____
Number 3 _____	_____ _____ _____	_____ _____ _____

SUMMARY

- Leaders and followers agree that good decision making is a primary criterion for successful leadership.

- Most people can improve their decision-making skills through the use of a system or procedure that employs logic. However, a procedure can only lead to a better decision; it cannot make it.

- Leaders are respected when they make the best possible decision in a quick, decisive manner.

- Leadership is often transmitted as much by the way a decision is announced as the decision itself.

- There is a high correlation between good decision making and the kind of leadership image transmitted.

- The group decision-making process should be followed as long as it leads to better decisions.

- It is better to correct a bad decision than to live with it.

Decision Making

Practicing with a logical process like the one below can improve the quality of your decisions. You are therefore encouraged to use it now to solve your number-one problem. First, review the model illustrated on page 87. Next, write out your answers step by step in the spaces provided. Continue using this process to solve major problems for the next thirty days.

Process	*Answers*
Define the desired outcome.	_____
Establish decision criteria.	_____
	_____
	_____
Come up with alternative solutions.	_____
	_____
	_____
Investigate—get all possible facts.	_____
	_____
	_____
Settle on top three choices.	_____
	_____
	_____
Instigate a comparison.	_____
	_____
	_____
Opt for the best choice.	_____
Notify those involved with decisiveness.	
See that decision is fully implemented.	

Case 11: Viewpoint

Al Bello is a paid United Fund leader. Jessica James is the owner of her own business. They are good friends and frequently get together to discuss their successes and failures. "I've been agonizing over my decisions for over 20 years," claims Al Bello, "and frankly I believe I should have devoted more time to announcing and articulating my decisions and less time to making them. I believe you can make a so-so decision and providing you announce it with decisiveness, conviction, and strength, it may accomplish more than a better decision announced in a more routine matter. Does this make sense?"

"I agree,"Jessica replies, "that announcing and articulating a decision in a forceful manner is important, but nothing can take away the sting of a bad decision, or even a poor one. Sooner or later the quality of your decisions will catch up to you. My decisions are designed to keep my company in a profit mode so that my employees will continue to work enthusiastically. If I make a decision that disrupts this pattern, I'm in trouble, no matter how much attention and power I put behind the announcement."

"I'm not so sure the quality of one's decisions means that much," states Mr. Bello. "There is a time-lag element. By the time those involved can tell whether a good or bad decision has been made, they have forgotten who made it. Or they don't care. In the future I'm going to make the best possible decision without spending so much time and then spend more time implementing it. If my subordinates think I am a good leader, they will go along with my decisions, good or bad. We should use decisions to communicate our leadership, not our logic."

"I can't follow your rationale on this," Jessica responds. "You are a good leader if you make good decisions. This is true because you are leading in the right direction. The fact that others may not know you are making sound decisions is not as important as your knowing it. And, besides, sooner or later all decisions come back to haunt you. I know."

Which viewpoint would you support? Is there such a thing as a decision time lag? Do we hold our leaders responsible for their decisions? Is the decision-making process overestimated as a leadership essential? (The author's comments are given in the back of the book.)

Members of the board of trustees for a small, private foundation are engaged in writing up the criteria for the selection of a new president. The previous president left the organization in shambles because of a series of poor decisions.

Three board members agree that it would be a good idea for anyone submitting an·application to also submit a decision-making track record. The record would include a list of major decisions made over the past five years, the applicant's assessment of why they were good decisions, and verification from a responsible party that the decisions turned out well for all concerned. Anyone who does not submit such a track record will not be considered.

The remaining two trustees take an opposing view. They believe it is impossible to verify whether a decision is good or bad, that many highly qualified leaders would not submit applications because of this special requirement, and that it is virtually impossible to determine ahead of time the decision-making capabilities of an applicant.

Which group would you support? What suggestion might you make to help them select a good decision maker without having each applicant submit a track record? Do you feel the board is placing too much emphasis on decision making to the detriment of other more important characteristics? (Turn to the back of the book to read the author's opinion.)

Case 12: Decision

Self-Test

Mark each statement below True or False.

_____ 1. Improving your decision-making ability is a good way to put more leadership into your style.

_____ 2. The way you announce and articulate a decision has little to do with the leadership image you communicate.

_____ 3. Subordinates keep accurate records of the decisions their leaders make.

_____ 4. Good decision makers always follow the same, logical, prescribed procedure.

_____ 5. It is best to openly acknowledge bad decisions and make immediate corrections.

_____ 6. Following a standard decision-making process for 30 days can improve the quality of decisions for the inexperienced leader.

_____ 7. The group process invariably produces better and faster decisions.

_____ 8. A poor decision made with decisiveness can be better than no decision at all.

_____ 9. Decision making does not bother leaders as much as followers.

_____ 10. There is no such thing as a "gut decision."

Turn to the back of the book to check your answers.

TOTAL CORRECT _____

Chapter 7

Establish Yourself as a Positive Force

It is a time for a new generation of leadership to cope with new problems and new opportunities. For there is a new world to be won.

John Fitzgerald Kennedy

OBJECTIVES

After finishing this chapter, you will be able to:

• Take immediate steps to establish yourself as a more positive force.

• Improve the way in which you communicate this force to your followers.

• Understand the need for a two-level communications network.

Mary started her first season as a girl's soccer coach naive, nervous, and with little hope of success. Only a few girls had turned out, and they were an undisciplined bunch. Her heart sank as she watched the first day's practice.

But Mary was determined that things would improve. Because of her positive attitude, she soon built a happy relationship with each player. The girls began to have fun at practice, and after winning a few games, they started building skill, confidence, and poise. When Mary told her fellow high school coaches that she intended to win the conference title, they laughed. But when the season was over her team had the trophy to prove it.

Mary is no ordinary coach. She knows that most leaders have many enviable personal characteristics: Most are intelligent, perceptive, personable, self-motivating, and courageous. She doesn't downplay these traits, but she knows that there is one other critical trait that most people never think of when describing leadership.

It is the ability to create a positive force.

In contrast to the other coaches, Mary had created, communicated, and maintained a consistent positive force. Her girls, without knowing it, were caught up in something that made them reach beyond their true potential as competitors. It was this force that had made the difference in their season.

WHAT IS A POSITIVE FORCE?

In one sense, it is nothing more than positive expectations. But, in another, it is a dynamic force that emanates from a leader and pulls the entire group into an inner circle of involvement and activity. Once it gets started, it seems to generate vigor and confidence. It stirs people up. It motivates. It removes obstacles. It leads to constructive action. It is, in effect, a form of energy. It gets people on the right track and keeps them moving. It stems from the positive attitude of the leader, but it manifests itself in action. Once a positive force gets under way, there is a group psychology that takes over. Like a cyclone or tornado, it picks up momentum. Although it seems to feed on itself, the increased velocity comes from the dynamics (contributions) of the members of the group. It is difficult to stand on the sidelines and not be drawn into it.

When there is an absence of positive leadership, lethargy takes over. The sensation of motion disappears. Lassitude prevails. The organization or group becomes sluggish and fat. Group members are left uninspired, and ultimately disenchanted.

When leadership does not generate a positive force, those required to exist inside organizational frameworks usually relax, mark time, and take the course of least resistance. Without the positive force, the organization loses its life.

HOW DO YOU CREATE A POSITIVE FORCE?

Leaders create the force in their own individual ways, as the figure on the next page illustrates. They glamorize their role positions, making them the center of action. They turn their personality power loose, sending rays of energy in all directions. They show personal vigor; they demonstrate a bearing that communicates strength. They create the feeling that something good is about to happen.

Like a pebble dropped into a quiet pool, the power of your own positive attitude starts the force, but it is your own special characteristics that push it into wider and wider circles. Each leader must develop his own centrifugal-power configuration, employing all positive personality characteristics and elements to keep the force alive.

But it all starts with a positive attitude.

Remaining positive under trying conditions is not an easy task. Yet, if you wish to be a successful leader you have no choice. You must remain positive because your positive attitude is the source of the power. Your positive attitude communicates to those you lead that they are headed in the right direction, that there are exciting goals within reach, that something better lies over the horizon. A positive attitude in a leader builds positive expectations in the minds of the group, whereas a negative attitude destroys them. When a leader turns negative the positive force dissipates as quickly as the air in a punctured balloon.

Establishing Yourself as a Positive Source

AS A LEADER YOU ARE ALWAYS ON CENTER STAGE

Because leaders transmit much of their positive force through their presence or personality, they must always put their best foot forward. They must always be in charge. They must always be up so that their followers will never feel down.

"I can let my negative feelings show to my secretary and immediate staff, but never to my employees."

"You can never let down in front of the troops."

"When I'm not up, neither is the team."

"Leadership and being positive are inseparable."

"I need the weekend on the ranch so I can come back Monday and be positive again."

Being constantly on stage can make or break a leader, especially in the world of politics, where the pressure is intense. But this kind of visibility also exists for coaches, corporate leaders, youth workers, ministers, and many others who occupy leadership roles. Whatever your leadership position may be, now or in the future, this responsibility will have more meaning to you after you complete the exercise on the following page.

PERSONALITY AND VOICE POWER

Personality power plays a leading role in the development of a positive force. When I interviewed leaders, their body language told me immediately that they were take-charge people. I could feel the force of their personalities as I entered their offices. In fact, at times it seemed as if I had walked into a magnetic field.

Their grooming, diction, and bearing communicated personal power, but looking back, nothing was more impressive than their voices. The tone and the manner in which they talked communicated a positive force. I could tell they were deliberately using their voices to impress me with their leadership strength. It worked because to a measurable degree personality power is voice power, and to a measurable degree positive force begins with the voice of the leader.

PERSONAL ACTIVITY CONTRIBUTES TO A POSITIVE FORCE

Successful leaders are always on the move. They transfer their positive attitudes into physical action. They create a flurry of activity that has a domino effect. It sets the tempo for others to follow.

Leaders operate in the sea of activity they create themselves and then watch it flow throughout their organization. This is the way one executive secretary describes her boss, a recognized leader.

> "The only time you will find things peaceful around here is when she is on a trip. She thrives on activity and it's catching. I sometimes feel I'm in the center of a hurricane. Everyone here at the home office knows immediately when she is back from a trip. In fact, we feel the storm coming ahead of time."

MOTIVATIONAL DELEGATING

There are two kinds of delegating. One form is designed to get work done—to meet production schedules and so on. In the other form, motivational delegating, leaders assign research, ask

Press Conference

In order to establish yourself as a positive force, you must communicate the impression that you are in charge whenever you are in the presence of others. To help you learn to do this, assume you are the subject of a televised press conference. All eyes are on you as you walk into the studio.

List in order of priority the specific impressions you would like to project to your audience by placing (in the left column) the number 1 next to the characteristic you feel most important, and so on, down the line. In the right-hand column, rank in order of priority the characteristics you need to work on the most.

Priority		*Work Needed*
_____	imperturbability	_____
_____	positive attitude	_____
_____	vigor	_____
_____	positive bearing	_____
_____	friendliness	_____
_____	excellent speaking ability	_____
_____	good grammar and diction	_____
_____	knowledgeability	_____
_____	sincerity-honesty	_____
_____	sense of humor	_____
_____	good grooming	_____
_____	decisiveness	_____

You can now match your numbers under each category. If you discover that you have entered a low number (high priority) on both sides of a single factor, any improvement you make in this area will pay double dividends in creating a stronger in-charge impression.

for reports, and seek advice. They constantly keep people involved by giving them something new to do to keep them from getting bored. Motivational delegating helps people reach their potential. Not that the tasks delegated do not need to be accomplished. Most of them do. The idea is that they keep people moving, creating and releasing their talent and energy. This kind of delegating enhances the positive force that is already alive. It keeps life in the group or organization. Leaders seem to sense that this kind of delegating is an extension of their own, personal force.

"I motivate my people almost 100 percent through delegation. I cook up ideas that can't help but have a positive thrust—and then I turn them over to others. I never want anyone on my staff to ever catch up and relax. They wouldn't be happy if this occurred."

"It's my responsibility as a leader to keep everyone moving, living at their capacity, contributing. I hate boredom myself, and it really galls me to see my people idle. So if they don't have enough to do, I create it."

"Inactivity always leads to trouble. I do not want my employees to live in a stressful climate, but I want them busy at all times. I will resort to anything in the book to make this happen."

It is obvious that coaches cannot wait around for their teams to catch fire; executives cannot sit back and wait for their employees to pick themselves up; ministers cannot expect their congregations to provide their own spiritual guidance; and community leaders cannot expect volunteers to motivate themselves. Leaders must step in and make these things happen. Motivational delegating is the prime tool in their kits.

Once created, how can the positive force be kept alive? Once there is movement, how can it be maintained?

The answer is communication.

Without good communication, a positive force cannot get started in the first place, let alone thrive. The leader must set up and maintain an effective organizational communications network. Without it, the positive force will die in the leader's office.

A communications network keeps a leader in touch with the people he or she leads. It can include every kind of medium—

MAINTAINING MOMENTUM THROUGH A COMMUNICATIONS NETWORK

from a personal note to a slick house organ, from a simple telephone call to a nationally televised public affairs program. A network is a media system that allows members of a group to be in on the action and leaders to keep in touch with the feelings of the group when personal contact is impossible. A good network can keep everyone in tune with organizational goals. Members of the group know where they are, why they are doing what they are doing, and what may happen down the road. They feel they belong.

THE FORMAL COMMUNICATIONS NETWORK

Every organization, large or small, has its own formal communications system. The following case illustrates how extensive such a system can be.

> Peter Gomez is the newly hired president of the XYZ corporation. XYZ used a headhunting firm to find its new leader because the poor performance of its previous president convinced the board the firm needed new blood. A new, fresh, positive force might put some life back into the firm. When Mr. Gomez arrived, his first priority was to analyze the existing communications network. A total revamping was called for. Within 30 days, Mr. Gomez had accomplished the following: (1) He replaced the communications officer; (2) he set up a series of meetings; (3) he wrote the lead article for the next issue of the house publication; (4) he purchased video equipment for the training department and prepared six tapes to be shown to all employees; (5) he scheduled one personal tour a week to cover all 11 departments in the organization; (6) he initiated a weekly bulletin outlining key developments of the past week to be distributed to all employees every Monday morning; (7) he set aside every Friday afternoon from 3 to 5 for informal chats with employees; (8) he asked his new communications officer to restyle the house publication; (9) he increased the communications budget.
>
> Although Mr. Gomez knew that he would not be able to maintain such a flurry of activity over a sustained period of time, he decided it was necessary to launch a positive force that would eventually turn the organization around. Without the new, revised communications network, this could not have been accomplished.

Personal Contract—Observer Verification

It is possible to become a more positive force in any imaginable leadership role—as a parent or a community volunteer. In this exercise, you make a contract with yourself to demonstrate you can be a more positive force in the future. This means you will need to increase your enthusiasm and generally communicate a more positive posture and attitude. The procedure recommended is as follows.

STEP 1. Find a suitable observer—someone who sees you in operation on a daily basis. Your boss, a colleague, a mentor, a friend, or family member will do. Make sure it is a person you respect and one who is familiar with your behavior patterns.

STEP 2. Take this person to lunch or dinner and explain that you have made a contract with yourself to extend your positive influence into wider circles. You are sincere in your desire to improve your leadership style. The reason for a structured meeting is to make certain the contract is not interpreted as a temporary or offhand decision.

STEP 3. At the meeting, ask the individual if she or he will observe the way you behave during a 30-day period. Ask him (or her) to tell you at the end of this period if he can sense any behavior modifications that indicate you are acting in a more positive manner. The individual can make mental or written notes during the period, but should not talk to you about the experiment or tell anyone else about it.

STEP 4. Tear out or make a copy of the figure on page 106 and place it on your refrigerator door or other appropriate place where it will remind you of the contract you have made.

STEP 5. At the end of the 30-day period, set up a second meeting to discuss results. Were behavior changes noticeable? Did others not involved in the experiment notice? Were all changes an improvement? What can be done to keep the positive force alive in the future?

STEP 6. Evaluate the observer's comments and make a long-term contract for continued improvement.

SETTING UP A DOUBLE NETWORK

A single communications network is inadequate to maintain and project a positive force. One leader expressed the need for a double network in this manner.

"I work hard to keep my formal communications network in good repair and operating smoothly, but I cannot depend upon it 100 percent. I must also maintain a highly personal, backup system both to transmit messages and to keep me informed on what is really going on."

The purpose of an informal system is to provide the leader with a supplemental network—a secondary system that permits the leader to communicate with his people on a more impromptu basis.

William Jackson, president of a nationwide industrial concern, was proud of his formal communications network. It accomplished what he had intended it to do. He spent equal time, however, on his informal system. He did this not because he was suspicious of others but because the formal system was, by definition, slow and traditional. Therefore, he was constantly on the telephone or making surprise visits throughout the country. Here are his comments: "My informal system permits me to keep everyone on their toes. They never know when they will hear from me. You see, I want them to feel my presence even if I am not there. It's my job to keep this outfit alive and moving. As their leader, it is the most important contribution I make."

NEGATIVE COUNTERFORCES

A well known entertainer purchased an expensive fur coat at an exclusive boutique in Las Vegas. She then asked to use the telephone to call her insurance agent to make arrangements to have the fur insured immediately. As she hung up the telephone she remarked to the salesperson, "I need the fur for my image, but I've got to recognize it might be ripped off at any moment."

Leaders have something of the same problem. They must create and maintain an image, but they must accept the fact that some members of the group might, at any time, turn against them. They cannot, unfortunately, purchase insurance for protection, but they must constantly be aware that a disenchanted subordinate might try to undermine them. This, too, goes with leadership territory.

A good, two-level, two-way communications network has a critical secondary purpose. In addition to transmitting the positive force created by the leader, it must also uncover potentially dangerous counterforces so that some form of corrective action can be taken before things get out of hand.

Mary Mullins, mayor of a community of over fifty thousand residents, was determined to cut down on crime. To this end, she beefed up the resources of the police department. Her efforts paid off handsomely, but other city employees, especially those in the fire department, started to feel neglected and even hostile. Fortunately, Mrs. Mullins received a signal through her communications system that all was not well. She immediately set up a meeting with the fire chief, started to visit outlying stations, and got the local newspaper to run a series of feature articles on the work of the fire department. Her communications system came to her rescue before things got out of hand.

The moment you make the transition to a leadership position, you become a potential target. You lose the anonymity you enjoyed as a member of the group. You become a topic of conversation around coffee tables, locker rooms, and public bars.

As a member of a group, you were secure. You had more freedom, fewer responsibilities, and time to relax and enjoy your colleagues. As a leader, you must try to provide the rewards the members of the group desire, but you have less security yourself. You also have less time and opportunity for casual conversations. Everything suddenly becomes more formal. You find yourself dependent upon your communication systems.

It is easy to see why top political leaders have press agents and public relations specialists to help them create and monitor the positive force that keeps them in office. Even with the assistance they receive, they frequently get into trouble.

If you are a first-line supervisor, a middle manager, a coach, or a volunteer leader, you may not have a staff surrounding you to provide this communications assistance and protection. You may have to make it a do-it-yourself project. In doing this, you too may discover that it is far easier to create positive momentum than to keep it going.

Whatever leadership role you may now occupy or will assume in the future, if you wish to be successful over the long term you must accept the challenge of creating and maintaining a positive force.

To neglect it is leadership suicide.

SUMMARY

- You cannot exist long as a leader without developing a positive force that will inspire those who follow you.

- A positive force generates constructive action.

- Like the other foundations upon which it rests, a positive force is part of the essence of leadership.

- Such a force stems from a positive attitude, which is at the heart of your personality power.

- You must discipline yourself to be on stage at all times.

- A good, sophisticated communications system permits the leader of a large organization to communicate his or her positive force to members of the group no matter how far away they may be.

- A secondary, informal network is needed to keep the leader informed of negative counterforces.

Leadership Comparison Exercise—Positive Force

In this exercise you are to measure and rate your three models on their abilities to generate a positive force within their respective groups. Some leaders are far better at this than others, so you should have little trouble in making your evaluations. Please ask yourself these questions.

- Are you, as a subordinate or observer, caught up in the positive force created by this leader? Can you sense its presence?

- Has this leader created a dynamic, positive group acceptance of his or her leadership to the point that members of the group are totally motivated to follow?

- Is this leader aware that he (or she) is constantly on stage, or is he sometimes negative or apathetic?

- Do you, under this leader, feel you are going somewhere? Is the organization moving? Is there an upbeat feeling in the group?

- Would you be willing to follow this leader in the face of strong opposition from others?

- Does this leader make it easy for you to stay positive?

	Strong Points	*Weak Points*
Number 1 _____ *(best at creating a positive force)*	_____ _____ _____	_____ _____ _____
Number 2 _____	_____ _____ _____	_____ _____ _____
Number 3 _____	_____ _____ _____	_____ _____ _____

Case 13: Charisma

Justine and Rebecca have been good friends since college days, when both prepared for careers in youth work. Justine is currently director of a YMCA in Northern California. Rebecca is a Girl Scout executive for a large council in Southern California. Both are attending a leadership seminar sponsored by a nationally known foundation. They are sitting around the dinner table discussing the importance of creating and maintaining a positive force. Justine comments:

"My observation tells me that charisma is the primary source of a positive force. This is especially true in youth activities, because kids are so impressionable. If kids are to respond, there has to be a touch of magic in the leader's personality—a something that makes the leader a model. Without this, it's impossible for leaders to establish themselves as a moving force."

"You say that," replies Rebecca, "because you are long on charisma, and you rely on it. What about plain Janes like me? Can we never be leaders just because we are not blessed with charisma? I believe we can lead if we develop good, positive attitudes. That is what young people want in a leader. Someone who looks at the good side and transmits confidence. Attitude is the answer, not charisma."

Do you support Justine or Rebecca? Why? Could you build a case that a positive attitude is a charismatic characteristic? (The author's opinion is given in the back of the book.)

Fred Fisher, executive vice-president of a large utility, and Jane Grey, public relations officer for the same firm, are having lunch in the executive dining room.

"I agree with the positive force idea," states Fred, "and we are fortunate to have J. B. as our president. He really stays positive, moves around, and somehow provides us with the vision and force we need to keep growing. He is a remarkable leader and certainly makes my job easier."

"In a way that is true," replied Jane, "but the positive force he represents still needs to be communicated to our nine thousand employees, our stockholders, and customers. He cannot do this alone. In fact, it is about 10 percent effort on his part and 90 percent effort on our part. I agree he has a good image for us to transmit, but we still have to do it. He still needs to be sold in every publication, on television, and in all media. You might say he creates a positive force but we communicate it."

"You may be overstating your own importance. I believe the lowest employee we have would feel the positive force he creates without any formal communications. A positive force is personality-based, and it transmits itself more through the grapevine and personal contact than through the media. One employee catches it and passes it on to another. You're saying, in effect, that you manufacture the positive force that keeps this company moving."

"No, I'm saying that without a well-organized formal communications system, any positive force created by the top leader would eventually die on the vine. J. B. couldn't get his positive force beyond you and his personal staff without us. We enhance, maintain, and protect his image. We keep the force going."

"I'm not saying we should eliminate the PR department," said Fred, "but you totally underestimate how much J. B. does on his own."

Does Ms. Grey overstate her case? Does Mr. Fisher underestimate the importance of formal communications? Take a position on the problem and defend it. (The author's reaction is given in the back of the book.)

Case 14: Communi- cations

Self-Test

Mark each statement below True or False.

_____   1. A positive force emanates from a leader and pulls followers into an inner circle of involvement.

_____   2. Without a positive force created by leaders, the members of a group will take the course of least resistance.

_____   3. Everyone has the capacity to create a force that people will follow.

_____   4. A positive attitude is the primary source of a positive force.

_____   5. It is not advisable for leaders to use their three sources of power to create a positive force.

_____   6. A positive force automatically transmits itself throughout an organization.

_____   7. The stronger the positive force, the more likely a negative counterforce will surface.

_____   8. The fact that the positive force foundation is at the top of the pyramid means that it is most important.

_____   9. Leaders, whether they know it or not, are always on center stage.

_____   10. Nonleaders have the luxury of being negative; leaders do not.

Turn to the back of the book to check your answers.

TOTAL CORRECT _____

Chapter 8

Articulate a Winning Mission

And if the blind lead the blind, both shall fall into the ditch.

Matthew 15:14

OBJECTIVES

After finishing this chapter, you will be able to:

- Explain the difference between a goal and a mission.

- Defend the premise that every organization or group, no matter how small, should have a winning mission.

On a recent flight to Washington, D.C., I sat next to a young Native American who was flying to the capital to accept a Small Business Administration award for starting a successful business to recycle steel slag. We touched on many subjects, but I was most impressed with how he interpreted the mission of his small company. "Our purpose is to live in harmony with the land—to use what we take, to return what we do not need. It is the Indian way." The goal of his company was to make money and survive; its mission was conservation of natural resources, and he knew exactly how to articulate it.

Peter Drucker, in his book *Managing for Results*,* discusses the importance of a single organization goal for both managers and employees. If such a goal exists (and is articulated), it could and should be converted into a mission. A mission has two purposes: It gives the whole organization (managers and employees alike) a sense of unity and purpose, and it keeps everyone moving with enthusiasm in the right direction.

Perhaps the following story will clarify, better than any explanation, the difference between a goal and a mission.

Years ago I taught a Sunday school class for junior high students. Our mission was to become better people by studying the principles of Christianity. Our goal was a yearly trip to nearby Disneyland. Unfortunately, to the children, the goal became more important than the mission: they could not see the forest (spiritual growth) for the trees (Disneyland).

The same thing happens in many organizations. Leaders put so much emphasis on short-term goals that they neglect to articulate a mission, which would, in the long run, be far more motivating to the group.

Let's look at a few more examples.

The goal of a YMCA group might be a two-week hike in the mountains. The mission might be to provide a group experience

---

*New York, Harper & Row, 1964.

that would teach self-reliance, cooperation, and other qualities important to the development of young adolescents.

A goal for an educational institution might be to upgrade the curriculum. The mission might be to prepare all students more adequately for their future roles in society.

A mission can be a rainbow in the sky; a goal a chore. A mission can be a dream or a vision; a goal a duty one is expected to perform. A mission provides meaning and self-fulfillment; a goal provides rewards that are soon forgotten. Generally speaking, a goal is more immediate, more pragmatic, and more mundane than a mission.

A goal, by definition, must be reachable; a mission need not. A mission does not have to be accomplished—and in fact may never be. But it must stir the imagination and feed the soul.

Many people complain that they do not feel good about the work they are doing. There is little personal gratification, little recognition, little glory. Perhaps it is because their leaders have not provided a sense of mission that would give their efforts some meaning. The leader who can create and articulate such a mission will always have followers.

LEADERS SUPPORT THE NEED FOR A GROUP MISSION

The mission symbol on the Leadership Formula is there because the leaders interviewed insisted it should be. Although many preferred the term "overriding purpose" to "mission," they were all enthusiastic about the idea the word represented. Providing a mission, in their opinion, is the essence of leadership.

There was also general agreement that creating the right mission and then articulating it is a major challenge. Their comments are both a measure of their enthusiasm for the idea and their personal struggles to make it work.

"Any leadership concept that does not include the responsibility of creating an overall purpose or vision is shallow indeed."

"The purpose of a mission is to provide direction, and direction is what leadership is all about."

"I agree with the mission idea, but it is easier for a minister or a politician to produce one than the head of a business organization."

"The most important thing a mission does is motivate the leader."

CONVERTING A PRIMARY GOAL INTO A MISSION

Sometimes a goal can be converted into a mission by following a procedure like this: (1) Isolate the three most important goals within the group or organization; (2) select the one that has the greatest appeal; (3) convert this goal into a mission by giving it a new, more dynamic title; and (4) articulate it in such a way that it stands above organizational goals.

Another way to come up with a suitable mission is through the technique of brainstorming. The leader calls some members of the group together and says, "What are we really trying to do here?" Often a mission will surface in the first session. The group technique makes sense because those who will carry out the mission should, if possible, be involved in creating it. If it doesn't stir their imaginations or give them a sense of pride, it is probably the wrong mission for that group. Of course, it is also important that the leader be committed to the mission. A good mission is often an extension of the leader—an integral part of his or her positive force.

The purpose of the following exercise is to help you test a current or proposed mission.

WINNING IS AN ACCEPTABLE MISSION

It is not always possible for a leader to create an ideal or original mission. But even if a leader can't create one that inspires or excites, all is not lost. The sense of pride that accompanies winning can be a good mission. Many times there is no need to look further. In this respect, coaches have a big advantage over other leaders. They have an automatic mission—winning! And best of all, every time they start a new season their sense of mission is renewed.

Winning is upbeat, exciting, and full of personal rewards. If you have ever participated in a sport, you may know the pride that comes from playing on a winning team. There is nothing quite like it. But teams are not the only organizations that win. It is a great feeling to be with a business organization that is making a profit and expanding (winning). It is a great feeling to work for an educational institution that has high standards and successful programs (winning); it is a great feeling to be on a police force that is admired and respected by the community it serves (winning).

Any type or size of organization or group can be a winner.

Finding A Mission

Please write down in the space provided a possible mission, and then answer the questions. If you have eight or more yes answers, it would appear you have designed a suitable mission for your group.

Mission: _____

		Yes	No
1.	Does this mission lead everyone in the group in the best possible direction?	☐	☐
2.	Will it benefit all members equally?	☐	☐
3.	Will it help to sustain and protect the organization over the long term?	☐	☐
4.	Can I, as a leader, articulate the mission clearly to all members of the group?	☐	☐
5.	Can the mission be converted to a slogan?	☐	☐
6.	Will the members of my group accept the mission with enthusiasm?	☐	☐
7.	Am I highly enthusiastic about it myself?	☐	☐
8.	Will the mission increase motivation appreciably?	☐	☐
9.	Is it sufficiently visionary to work?	☐	☐
10.	Is it the best possible mission under the circumstances?	☐	☐

THE PROBLEM OF ARTICULATION

Many leaders forget that it is as important to articulate a mission as it is to create one. They assume that if the mission is a good one it will survive on its own. They are wrong. A mission, to be successful, must be transmitted clearly and frequently through all available communications networks. If a mission can be encapsulated in a slogan or catch phrase, it is more likely to be remembered.

If the leader himself communicates the mission, it will also have greater impact. He should, without question, make communicating the mission the number-one priority in all talks to members of the group, either personally or on video tape. The more a mission is personalized by the top leader the better.

A few political pundits believe that President Reagan did not win the national election in 1980 because his mission was more acceptable to the majority of American people; he won because he did a superior job of articulating it. From the day he left the governorship of California to the day he won the election, Reagan accepted speaking engagements in every part of the United States. Not only did his mission (to return to a more conservative America) capture his audiences, it also became more and more motivating to the future President himself.

Some observers believe that the success of a mission depends more on articulation (90 percent) than on content (10 percent). They are quick to point out, for example, that making a profit is the true mission of any business enterprise. Yet this mission is never fully articulated. Workers are not reminded that if their firm does not win in the marketplace, their jobs are in jeopardy, that if the firm cannot make money, there will be no capital for growth, which in turn will create more career opportunities. As a mission statement, "make a profit" is probably inspiring only to those who benefit directly—stockholders and employees who participate in profit-sharing plans. But put another way, the profit motive can inspire all: "Keep your chin up, you're with a winner," or "when the company makes a profit we all win," are the kind of positive statements workers like to hear.

It is the responsibility of all leaders to lead the group in the direction that will provide the greatest benefit for all. But both benefit and direction must be understood by the group. If it is not, individual members may follow another course. It is only when leaders constantly communicate where they are going, why they are going there, and what it will mean when they arrive, that they are fulfilling their leadership potential.

Those leaders who abdicate the opportunity to establish and articulate a mission are letting both themselves and their followers down. They are backing away from the heart of leadership.

As the formula graphic illustrates, a winning mission becomes an extension of the positive force communicated by the leader. Although some good missions are the result of group consensus (recommended), most often leaders must create their own missions without help. After all, leaders do have the view from the top—the advantage of perspective.

In using their talents to come up with a mission, leaders must recognize that each group or organization—business, educational, government, religious, community—should create its own special mission. To copy the mission of another group is to miss the point. And a mission should always have the personal stamp of the leader. It should grow out of, and reflect, his or her positive force.

Superior leaders find much of their own personal motivation from the very missions they develop. Missions are, therefore, self-serving. They can, and often do, motivate the leader more than the followers.

Not a bad endorsement.

MISSIONS AND THE POSITIVE FORCE

Leadership Comparison Exercise—An Analysis

This exercise permits you to make a composite analysis of all five foundations for each of your three models. Please gather the scores from previous exercises and record them below.

Name of Model	Scores (1, 2, or 3) on Each Foundation					
	Communi-cation	MRT	Power	Decisions	Positive Force	Total

Did any model rate low (3) on all five foundations? Did any model rate high (1) on all foundations? Did one model rate high on one foundation and low on others? If so, how do you explain the discrepancies? Based upon your ratings, which of the three leaders would you prefer to model yourself after?

Based upon your analysis and interpretation, what specific suggestions would you make to each of the models—suggestions that would further strengthen them as leaders?

Suggestions

Number 1 _____   _____

Number 2 _____   _____

Number 3 _____   _____

Now that you have gone through the comparison process and become familiar with the five foundations, please answer the following questions.

• In your opinion, are the foundations valid? Explain.

_____

_____

_____

• Will you continue to use them to evaluate leaders? If so, why?

_____

_____

_____

• Does using the foundations help you at separating substance from style? Explain.

_____

_____

_____

• Did using the foundations as criteria produce results different from those you anticipated?

_____

_____

_____

• After rating your models on the five foundations, are they still, in your opinion, good models?

_____

_____

_____

• Are you more or less enthusiastic about weaving the foundations into your own style?

_____

_____

_____

SUMMARY
- A mission should be an extension of the positive force created by the leader.
- A mission is more than a goal. It reflects the overriding purpose of the organization or institution. It must inspire both leaders and followers.
- A mission has two purposes: to hold a group together and to head them in the right direction.
- Sometimes a primary organizational goal can be converted into a mission.
- Leaders often motivate themselves with their own missions.

Writing Mission Statements

Leaders who create their own missions are usually more enthusiastic about them. And if a mission can be encapsulated in a slogan, or mission statement, it is easier to communicate. With these two factors in mind, you are invited to try your hand at creating a mission statement for each of the following situations. When you are finished, you might enjoy comparing your statements with those of your fellow students (if you are part of a seminar or class).

You are the director of fund-raising for a private college. Your goal is to raise one million dollars, a 20-percent jump over last year. Write out a mission statement in the space below.

_____

_____

You are a high school coach. Your goal is to be conference champion. Write out a mission statement that will contribute to your goal.

_____

_____

As a corporate president, you are seeking a mission statement that will improve the image of your organization as well as contribute to higher profits. Write your best effort below.

_____

_____

Case 15: Sub-Missions

Professor Robinson is a master teacher. His course on Leadership is extremely popular. Maria, an office manager at 26, is one of his more assertive students. After a lecture on the importance of mission to the leadership concept, Maria volunteered this comment:

"I can understand why top leaders need to create a mission to motivate subordinates and to keep the organization alive and moving in the right direction, but I think it should stop there. Those of us at the bottom who run small departments should spend our time carrying out the big missions sent down to us. Creating one of our own is a joke."

Professor Robinson answered: "Does this mean that as an office manager you could not benefit from a tailormade mission for just your employees? Isn't it possible that you could accept the company mission and at the same time create a smaller, but still effective one of your own? What I'm leading up to is this. Sometimes, a departmental mission will do more to create team spirit than a corporate mission handed down from above. You could try to be the most efficient department, most envied, or most friendly. If you succeeded, it would give the department an identity, and members would feel they belonged to a winner."

Maria replied: "Everyone in our outfit is goal-happy. I get so many goals handed down to me I don't have time to develop any special mission. It would just be another responsibility. Besides, my employees are too sophisticated—they just laugh at the idea."

Professor Robinson continued: "I believe that creating a mission might be highly motivating to you, Maria. You might be more enthusiastic about a little mission you created yourself than a big one that trickled down from above. I'm not so sure that a mission at the bottom of an organization is not a good idea. It might make as much sense as one from the top. And it might contribute to productivity more."

Assume that you are a member of the class and Professor Robinson calls on you for your opinion. How would you reply? Would you support Maria or the Professor? (The author's opinion is given in the back of the book.)

Ramon Garcia, a hospital administrator, developed a mission statement for the 140-bed facility he supervises: "Better care—lower prices." Mr. Garcia tried out his mission statement on both internal and community groups. It was a great success. He then suggested to Louise Loring, his director of Human Resources, that she ask all hospital managers to develop a mission statement of their own. Mr. Garcia was careful to explain that departmental missions should follow the general mission in theme and certainly not conflict with it.

Mrs. Loring is a believer in participatory management. She quickly called a conference of the 16 managers representing various medical and nonmedical services. In presenting the idea, she pointed out that establishing and maintaining a mission is a demonstration of good leadership. She also got the group to agree on the following: (1) Missions shall be expressed as short statements. (2) They must be accepted by the majority of departmental personnel. (3) They must be submitted within 15 days. (4) All slogans will be posted in a public place so that everyone will know the mission of each department. (5) A winner will be selected, and those in the winning department will receive an extra day off with pay.

How would you evaluate this approach? Do you think it will be successful? What changes would you make? (See the back of the book for the author's suggestions.)

Case 16: Involvement

Self-Test

Mark the statements below True or False.

_____   1. A goal and a mission are the same thing.

_____   2. There is little relationship between a mission and a positive force.

_____   3. Peter Drucker states that all organizations need a single organizational goal, or mission.

_____   4. Sometimes having too many goals makes it more difficult to have a single mission.

_____   5. Making a profit so that employees, customers, and stockholders come out ahead is a legitimate mission for a business organization.

_____   6. Winning in itself can be a mission.

_____   7. It is easier to create a mission than to articulate it.

_____   8. Goals can never be converted into missions.

_____   9. Some leaders prefer the term "overriding purpose" to "mission."

_____   10. A mission can be an adventure; a goal a chore.

Turn to the back of the book to check your answers.

TOTAL CORRECT _____

Chapter 9

How to Weave the Formula into Your Style

A critic is a man who knows the way but can't drive the car.

Kenneth Tynan

OBJECTIVES

After finishing this chapter, you will be able to:

• Select the best strategy to put more leadership into your style.

• Make a personal contract with yourself to complete it.

Henry and his partner, Jake, are having their regular morning meeting to discuss operational problems in their chain of restaurants. Today, the discussion centers on the problem of training managers.

"Ten years ago," Henry remarks, "we had the time and money to conduct in-house seminars and give our new managers a lot of personal help. Today, with tighter budgets, all we can do is establish the best possible working environment, provide the tools, and hope they will train themselves."

Jake agrees. "If those in our organization who want to be leaders are not self-motivated, there is little we can do to help them."

Henry and Jake have a point.

You could be a national political leader, a corporate executive, a first-line supervisor, a priest, or a community leader. You could also be on the sidelines, a student preparing to be a leader. Whatever your position, if you want to become a better leader and are not self-motivated, you are in trouble. That is the bad news.

The good news is that if you really want to put more leadership into your style, you can do so. The formula provides the tools that can make you a winner, just as long as you realize it is a do-it-yourself project.

How you go about weaving the Leadership Formula into your style will depend upon your past experience and the role you occupy. Mature leaders may opt to review the formula and then concentrate on sharpening the skills that have become rusty. In doing so, they can start from either the top or the bottom of the pyramid. New leaders and students should consider weaving the complete formula into their style—step by step.

Listed below are three strategies designed to help you weave the total concept into your style. Choose the one that will work best for you.

STRATEGY I

Step 1: Review the one-page Leadership Formula Summary on page 137.

Step 2: Tear the summary out of the book or reproduce it. Then tape it up somewhere (at home or at work) where you will see it frequently. It will act as a reminder that you have made a contract with yourself to go through the various steps in your efforts to put more leadership into your style.

Step 3: After 30 days, complete the Leadership Competency Checklist (pages 138—39) to measure the progress you have made.

STRATEGY II

Step 1 (Same as step 1 above.)

Step 2 (Same as step 2 above.)

Step 3: Instead of attempting to incorporate all foundations into your style at once, take each foundation one week at a time. (Make a checkmark next to each completed level in the Leadership Formula Summary as you move on from week to week.)

Step 4: After five weeks, complete the Leadership Competency Checklist (pages 138–39) to measure your progress.

STRATEGY III

Step 1: Make a photocopy of the Leadership Competency Checklist (pages 138—39) and take it to a superior, mentor, or another person who will agree to observe your leadership behavior over a five-week period. Tell this person that you are embarking on a project to put more leadership into your style and that you would like him (or her) to place a checkmark (and appropriate comments) next to any competency in which he has noted improvement.

Step 2 (Same as step 1 in Strategy I.)

Step 3 (Same as step 2 in Strategy I.)

Step 4 (Same as step 3 in Strategy II.)

Step 5: After five weeks, call the second party. Request that he (or she) complete the checklist you gave him earlier. Do the same yourself. Arrange a meeting where the two ratings can be compared. Discuss.

Leadership Formula Summary

FIFTH WEEK

Starting today, establish yourself as a more positive force. Develop a more positive personality by becoming more active, doing more motivational delegating, and improving your on-stage image. Assume responsibility for transmitting your new force to all members of the group.

FOURTH WEEK

Start paying more attention to the decisions you make. Improve the decision-making process you now use, or develop one that is even more effective. Become noticeably more decisive in announcing decisions. If you make a bad decision, take immediate corrective action.

THIRD WEEK

Start today to express your leadership qualities more emphatically. Do this by adjusting your authority line if necessary. Deal with current violations in a firm but sensitive manner. Use your role, personality, and knowledge power with more assurance.

SECOND WEEK

Start today to build a stronger human-relations base with members of your group. Do this by practicing MRT. If you have managers who report to you, teach them to do the same. When appropriate, employ MRT counseling. Continue to practice MRT as you move up the pyramid.

FIRST WEEK

Effective immediately, become a more sensitive listener and a more effective one-on-one and small-group communicator. Improve your large-group speaking skills. Start taking advantage of all opportunities to monitor and improve your communication skills.

Leadership Competency Checklist

A competency is a skill, technique, or attitude that can be demonstrated. You can observe leadership competencies in any group setting where there is a designated or volunteer leader. Although not as easy to identify or measure as technical or manipulative skills, leadership competencies are significantly more important to the success of the group. Listed below are the most important competencies discussed in this book. Once you feel that you have woven the skill, technique, or attitude into your behavioral pattern, place a check in the square provided.

Measurably strengthen your leadership ability by improving these communication skills.

☐ Become a better listener.

☐ Improve your one-on-one communication techniques.

☐ Train yourself to become more effective as a small-group leader.

☐ Develop your platform speaking skills.

Demonstrate that you can maintain the loyalty of the people you lead by providing the right rewards.

☐ Improve your human-relations base by using MRT as a counseling tool.

☐ Build better personal reward systems with the people you work with every day.

☐ Discover and provide better general rewards for group members with whom you have little or no personal contact.

Measurably strengthen your leadership image by using authority more competently and confidently.

☐ Set more consistent, more clearly defined authority lines.

☐ Correct violations immediately (and tactfully).

☐ Occupy your leadership position with more grace.

Leadership Competency Checklist
(*continued*)

☐ Increase your personality power by improving your weaker traits.

☐ Increase your knowledge power so that followers will automatically give you more respect.

Improve your decision-making skills to the point where both superiors and subordinates will notice a significant difference.

☐ Make better decisions through an improved process.

☐ Make faster decisions.

☐ Announce them more decisively.

☐ Become more skillful at using the group process to make decisions.

Demonstrate to subordinates and superiors that you have measurably strengthened these leadership skills.

☐ Establish yourself as a more positive force.

☐ Make more things happen by being less desk-bound.

☐ Do more motivational delegating.

☐ Speak with more clarity and conviction.

☐ Project a stronger visual image.

☐ Develop and improve the use of both formal and informal communication networks.

☐ Improve your surveillance of negative counterforces and take immediate action to dissipate any discovered.

☐ Establish a single winning mission.

☐ Articulate this mission so that everyone in the group will follow with more enthusiasm.

Case 17: Emphasis

Because business has been bad, both Aaron and Rose have been stuck in their management positions for over three years. They both agree that the best way to move up is to put more leadership into their style.

Rose plans to do this in a dramatic fashion. Having carefully analyzed her personal style, she has decided to work hard on two parts of the formula and ignore the others.

First, she is going to tighten up her discipline line a notch and maintain it with more force. She feels it is time to demonstrate her leadership more emphatically. Second, through more group interaction, she intends to generate a more positive force within her department. She intends to keep it going by becoming more positive personally, more active, and more assertive in all of her dealings with others. She is going to be on center stage at all times.

Aaron, more conservative and cautious by nature, feels that each of the five foundations is equally important and wishes to achieve balance. He is fearful that if he tightens up his authority line without first making sure that his reward system is effective, he might get into trouble. He is also fearful that if he suddenly becomes more of a positive force, the reaction from others might be counterproductive. He intends to gradually upgrade himself in all five areas without calling attention to himself. He feels that this will be more effective in getting him a promotion.

Which strategy do you support? Defend your position. (The author's reactions are given in the back of the book.)

Janice is self-confident, capable, and ambitious—a high-energy person. She never does anything halfway; it is all or nothing. Janice switches from one self-improvement project to another at frequent intervals. Everyone envies her energy, enthusiasm, and creativity. Her colleagues have noticed, however, that her follow-through is not always what it should be. There is little structure in her department and her employees are the most undisciplined in the firm.

Jill is also self-confident, capable, and ambitious, and a planner. She goes about everything in a methodical, deliberate manner. Her follow-through is excellent. She shows great attention to detail. Most of her co-workers admire her low-key approach. Some, however, feel she needs to become more of a self-starter and to provide greater recognition to those who work for her.

Both Janice and Jill, after attending a leadership workshop, wish to incorporate the Leadership Formula into their respective styles.

Which, in your opinion, would be most successful? What kind of success would you predict for Janice? Jill? (The author's prediction is in the back of the book.)

Case 18: Prediction

Self-Test

Mark each statement below True or False.

_____   1. Most managers can expect personal help from their superiors in putting more leadership into their style.

_____   2. Strategy I is the most difficult and, as a result, will probably produce greater results.

_____   3. Those in nonleadership positions cannot apply any part of the Leadership Formula.

_____   4. Most people who start out to add more leadership to their style give up rather quickly without showing any measurable improvement.

_____   5. The Leadership Formula Summary is designed to be posted in a place where it can act as a visual reminder.

_____   6. One should be able to make noticeable progress in integrating the total formula into one's style within 30 days.

_____   7. It is better to weave one foundation into your style than none at all.

_____   8. Because all the foundations are interrelated, it can be dangerous to emphasize one at the expense of another.

_____   9. You can lead a manager to the leadership water but you can't make him drink.

_____   10. If you are successful in putting more leadership into your style, your superiors and subordinates will notice a positive difference in your behavior.

Turn to the back of the book to check your answers.

TOTAL CORRECT _____

Appendixes

When applied in counseling situations, the Mutual Reward Theory can be used to build strong new relationships, to strengthen older ones, and to restore impaired relationships. The key to success is an open discussion of the theory itself followed by a reevaluation of the existing reward system between the leader and the subordinate. When both parties have sufficient time and opportunity to discuss the reward system honestly, both usually come out ahead—and a better leader-follower relationship has been created. The following cases illustrate how MRT counseling can put more leadership into one's style.

MRT CASE 1

Joe and Mark's relationship, which was excellent to start with, has drastically deteriorated in recent weeks. Not only has Mark's personal productivity slumped, but his behavior has had a negative impact upon the productivity of others.

Joe is new as a supervisor, and he has had little experience in counseling problem employees. He nevertheless decides to initiate a series of three counseling sessions in his office with Mark. He schedules 40 minutes for the first session (so that there will no time pressure) and asks the telephone operator to hold his calls. Joe's big decision is to use the MRT approach.

In the first meeting, Joe does his best to create a nonthreatening atmosphere. For a few moments Joe and Mark exchange small talk, and then Joe says, "Mark, I am going to discuss the Mutual Reward Theory with you for a few minutes." He explains the theory and then says: "There are certain rewards I can give you, and certain rewards you can give me. I believe the reward system between us is currently out of balance. If you can write out the rewards you want, I will write out those I would like. We can compare them, and then, I believe, we can improve the exchange so that we both come out ahead. Are you willing to do this?"

The discussion lasted 30 minutes. Mark put his reward expectations out front—and so did Joe. After a few compromises and clarifications, both parties agreed to make every effort to honor the arrangement. From that point on Mark made a greater effort to be productive, and a second counseling session was not necessary. By using the MRT approach in an honest, practical way, Joe had rebuilt and improved the working relationship. *He had demonstrated his leadership.*

MRT CASE 2   Martin, a youth leader taking part in an extended training program (and a young man with high potential), was assigned to Sandra's department for 30 days. After Martin had been in Sandra's department for a week, she gave him a special assignment that involved some research and a written report. Although the report was turned in on time, it did not live up to Sandra's expectations. She invited him into her office.

"Martin, I realize you will be with me only two more weeks, but I feel strongly that you are coasting through your time with me. There is more to learn in my special area than you think; and if you do not learn it now, sooner or later it will hurt your career. Are you familiar with the Mutual Reward Theory? It simply states that when both parties in a working relationship have a good exchange of rewards, both come out ahead. I believe we can improve our reward system. The rewards I want to give you will help you in the future; the reward you can give me is to do something to help my department before you leave. Are you willing to discuss the idea?"

After a 40-minute discussion, Martin agreed he had misinterpreted his assignment and that there was time left for the reward exchange Sandra had suggested.

Through the MRT design, Sandra had greatly improved the relationship between the two parties, helped the progress of her department, and improved Martin's future. *She had demonstrated her leadership.*

MRT CASE 3   Molly has been an excellent manager for over eight years. Recently, however, her performance has begun to slip. Sam, her superior, decides to intervene. Molly and Sam talk things over in a relaxed manner at lunch. The dialogue brings to light two factors Sam had not known about. Molly is having trouble with her 16-year old daughter at home, and is beginning to feel that her future at work is limited because of her lack of formal education.

"Molly, as your boss, I can provide only certain rewards. One would be to transfer you to the day shift, which would give you more time to spend with your daughter. The other is to suggest you start taking night courses at the local university. And even if you don't take any college courses, I don't think you've gone as far as you can go with us. If you're willing to become self-motivated again, we can eventually open things up. Why don't you give some serious attention to the reward you want from me and the company. The primary reward we want from you is improved productivity from those who work for you and continued leadership on your part. If we can work out a balance, everyone will come out ahead. Come back to see me before Friday. I'm sure we can work out an arrangement that is rewarding to both of us."

Through open discussion of possible rewards, a productivity problem has been solved, and Molly is again satisfied and making a significant contribution.

Mike knew his political campaign was in trouble. Running for a seat in the state assembly, he started out with high hopes and what appeared to be sufficient support, but nothing was working as it should. Mike finally decided that much of the blame should be placed upon the shoulders of his campaign manager, Victor. Mike decided on a heavy counseling session with Vic, keeping in mind that Vic's real ambition was to complete his Ph.D. at a local university. (Vic's salary was minimal; he was doing the job mainly for experience.)

MRT CASE 4

"Vic, I know you are as disappointed about things as I am. I want to say right out that not all of the fault is yours—some is mine, and some should fall elsewhere. But it occurs to me that you may not be getting the personal rewards you seek, and my big reward—getting elected and establishing a wider political base for the future—is likely to go down the drain. I've done some thinking on the subject, and I have isolated two rewards I think you may want. I would like you to verify whether or not they are the ones that will motivate you to do more than you have in the past. Give you more exposure to the policy-making part of the campaign, which may help you in your academic work, and promise you that whether I am elected or not I will be happy to act as your mentor if you decide to give up research or teaching for a political career. What I want to have happen is for both of us to come out ahead. I want to be fair, and I want to be realistic. I do know this: without your full attention to the campaign—we only have six weeks left—my chances are not good.

Before the meeting was over, a mutually rewarding contract had been worked out. Neither made promises they could not keep; neither demanded more than was reasonable. From that moment on, the campaign was back on track.

Suggested Leadership Activities

(For individual or classroom use)

1. Select a local or national political leader and assume you are his or her confidant. The leader comes to you for analysis and assistance. Based upon what you now know about leadership, what suggestions would you make? What parts of the formula would you urge the leader to add to his or her style?

2. Your boss knows that you have been studying the subject of leadership. He or she comes to you for advice on how to become a better leader. List your suggestions and state why you have made them.

3. Complete a 10-page critique of the Leadership Formula. Where is it weak? Strong? What improvements would you make? Are you satisfied that the formula incorporates the five basics that constitute the essence of leadership? Do you have a replacement? An addition?

4. Make the most objective analysis of your own leadership style you can. Assume that you decide to weave the Leadership Formula into your style the way it is presented. Will the formula improve your style? Will it fill in voids? Write a short paper describing how the formula will work for you.

Author's Responses to Case Problems

The leadership cases presented at the end of each chapter in this book were designed to be springboards for individual thinking and discussion purposes. There are no "right" answers to any of the cases.

At this early stage, all leadership concepts are nebulous in nature. Until more research and experimentation takes place, different points of view should be encouraged.

The following answers, then, are nothing more than the author's opinion based upon his personal investigation and interviews. They should serve only as a guide to the independent thinking of the reader and the discussion leader.

CASE 1: CONFLICT

The author supports the premise that if an individual learns the fundamentals of leadership in one environment, he or she should be able to transfer them successfully to another. If Greg learned and practiced some fundamentals (like those presented in the formula) in the military, he should have little trouble adapting them to a banking environment. It would appear that Greg is confused between leadership style and fundamentals. He may be having trouble because he is attempting to transfer an authoritative military style to a participatory situation. The fundamentals would fit both styles. As Vicki suggests, if a student learns the leadership basics in the classroom, he or she should be able to take them into any environment.

CASE 2: POTENTIAL

The author, naturally, gives his support to Jim. Bob seems to feel he must take his winning style completely apart and rebuild it to incorporate the fundamentals. This is not the case. Bob can weave one or more fundamentals into his style without disrupting it. As he does this, it may be necessary to make minor adjustments and modifications, but that is as far as it need go. He will, however, improve and strengthen his present style because he will fill in the weak spots in his previous emphasis on fundamentals. Put another way, his effective style will improve because it will be based upon a stronger foundation. When Bob senses the difference between style and substance, his fears should dissipate.

CASE 3: CONTROVERSY

Professor Adams deserves support on the basis that good management practices are essential to good leadership, and non-business professors may not have this important background. The point is well taken, however, that management professors might spend too much time on management and not enough on leadership. Their prejudices might show so much that non-business students might drop the course. You can also build a case that nonmanagement professors might be able to see the total concept more clearly from where they stand. This would put them in the position to introduce experiences and cases of a more general nature.

Leadership courses have been neglected because not enough is known about the subject to provide the basis for a traditional college course. In addition, teachers have not been trained to teach leadership.

CASE 4: OPINION

Both Elgin and Samantha start from excellent positions. Elgin, with his management expertise, should be able to make a quick and easy transition providing he can move away from management and concentrate on leadership. Samantha, because of her actual leadership experiences, may grasp the management skills and fundamentals sooner because she knows they will help her be a better leader. The author, in this case, goes along with Samantha because he senses that Elgin will fight leadership ideas every step of the way. He will probably be more interested in defending the accepted value of management instead of taking a fresh look at leadership. Samantha, on the other hand, will accept them and weave them into her style without apparent conflict or indecision.

CASE 5: IMPROVEMENT

A formal course in public speaking would probably provide Ms. Blake with the most help if she took the course seriously, became involved, and stayed with it to the end. Additional live-audience experiences and practice with her video equipment would also help. It would also be beneficial for Ms. Blake to study other speakers and improve her own skills through comparative analysis.

There may be some exceptions to the ten-minute restriction, but generally speaking it is good advice. Most speakers needlessly belabor the points they want to make, frequently confusing and exhausting their audience in the process. Speakers who can convey their messages clearly and quickly and still inspire their audiences are hard to find. His emphasis on both verbal and visual exposure in the right combination is sound.

CASE 6: EXPOSURE

Ministers and all other religious leaders who incorporate MRT into their style will automatically strengthen their leadership because they will have better contact with their congregations and a better knowledge of their members' religious and non-religious needs. Ralph's compassion for others should make the adoption and application of MRT easy and more effective. Still, it is doubtful that this will happen, because he is not enthusiastic about it. Perhaps he does not sense a need to be a stronger leader or build better relationships with his congregation. He seems to be satisfied with things as they are. Unless he comes to the realization that MRT could help him serve God better, nothing will happen.

CASE 7: COMPASSION

The best way to convince oneself of the value of MRT is to actually use it and measure the results. Chances are therefore good that after Mr. Nelson and Mr. Castelletti work out a better reward system between themselves, Mr. Castelletti will become more enthusiastic. Mr. Castelletti's fear is understandable but not justified. It is a comfortable approach to improving relationships and can be used in any environment with any style. Mr. Castelletti needs to be convinced that it will work as well for him, using his own approach, his own words, and that it is not just a technique for psychologists. Receiving the right rewards is as important to truckers as anyone else.

CASE 8: FEAR

Gloria may be a little optimistic about her chances of turning Jane into a forceful leader, but it is a real possibility. Assertiveness training seminars in recent years have clearly demonstrated this can happen. Nobody is born to be either a follower or a leader. In this area, one can be what one wants to be. This is not to say that anyone can become President of the United States, but it

CASE 9: COURAGE

does say that anyone who wants to be a local PTA or church leader can become one. Jane, with Gloria's help, can develop the courage to stand up to others. She can learn to apply structure. The very fact that Gloria sees Jane in the role as her assistant is a positive indication that the potential is there.

CASE 10: COMPATIBILITY

Captain Small builds an excellent case that MRT and structure are not only compatible but mutually dependent upon each other. One works much better when the other is present. This is perhaps even more true in the military than in less structured environments. In short, the more structure required, the more MRT is needed. Any military officer who can build a disciplined fighting unit on a sound human-relations platform is going to be a successful, respected leader.

The author is convinced that the more a leader uses MRT, the easier and more effective the application of structure becomes. When a subordinate is receiving the right rewards, he or she will accept structure because structure protects and continues the reward system. Both parties come out ahead. Of course it is possible to be a compassionate leader in the modern military establishment.

CASE 11: VIEWPOINT

Both viewpoints deserve support. Mr. Bello makes a strong point when he states there is a time lag between when decisions are made and when they are judged good or bad. Unfortunately, because of this we seldom have knowledge of the decision-making track records of our leaders. Ms. James is also right when she states that a poor decision can come home to haunt a leader. This is always a risk as every long-term leader has discovered. None of the leaders I interviewed thought the formula overstated the importance of decision making; some, however, suggested that it be given more weight among the five basic foundations. The term "the buck stops here" emerged in many conversations, an indication that leaders know they live with the pressure of making decisions. This responsibility may keep many people away from assuming leadership roles.

The author strongly supports the two trustees who believe it is most difficult to verify the decision-making ability of an applicant. As far as submitting their track records in advance, it is naive to think that they would not construct them to make themselves look good. The best way to gain insight into the decision-making capabilities of an applicant would be to ask the following questions during the interview stage: "How important is decision making to leadership?" "Do you feel you are a good decision maker? Why?" "Do you have a tested process you follow in making decisions? What is it?" Answers to these questions should be most revealing and would provide the interview board with the data they need on this vital subject. Is the board placing too much emphasis on decision making? Absolutely not! The destiny of any foundation is determined more by the quality of decisions than any other factor.

CASE 12: DECISION

Although charisma can be an irreplaceable asset to a leader, especially in the political arena, it is not essential. A leader with charisma may communicate a positive force more easily, but a positive force can be established without it, as Rebecca states. In fact, some leaders lean so heavily on charisma that they ignore the other, more powerful elements necessary to establish a positive force. It would be difficult, perhaps impossible, to build a case that a positive attitude is a charismatic characteristic. Charisma is a mix of traits that communicates a certain magic to followers; attitude is the way the leader looks at things mentally. Group members respond enthusiastically to any leader who has a positive attitude, perhaps because they want to believe in their leaders and the direction they are being asked to take. A charismatic leader may provide excitement, but a positive leader provides hope. The combination of both is, of course, ideal.

CASE 13: CHARISMA

It would appear that Ms. Grey overestimates the importance of communications in transmitting J.B.'s positive force; on the other hand, Mr. Fisher may be underestimating the role of public relations. It is impossible to say how far the positive force of a

CASE 14: COMMUNICATIONS

leader can be transmitted personally and when the communication network should take over. The leader of a small group (Boy Scout leader) may not need any help from a formal communications system, but the President of the United States needs all the help available. The balance required between the two is probably determined by the size of the group and the number of members who may be located some geographical distance away. A utility with 9000 employees certainly needs a two-level, two-way communications network if the positive force of the leader is to reach everyone. By the same token Ms. Grey is lucky to have a leader who does so much on his own.

**CASE 15:
SUB-MISSIONS**

It would be ideal if the leader of a sizable organization could create and communicate an overriding purpose (mission) that would be so powerful and involving that it would preclude the need for separate departmental missions. In such a situation, sub-missions might even do more harm than good. It might be a mistake, however, to say that smaller groups within the framework of a large organization should not have the opportunity to develop missions of their own. A primary purpose of a mission is to make a group more cohesive, provide direction, and furnish an identity. If smaller organizations like churches, ball teams, and volunteer groups can benefit from the creation of a mission as opposed to a goal, then it makes sense that individual branches, divisions, or departments within a large organization could also benefit. The author supports both views but leans more in the direction of the professor because it would be a mistake to discourage departmental managers from giving serious thought to a mission for their employees. What if the top leader of the organization has failed to come up with a motivating mission?

**CASE 16:
INVOLVEMENT**

Although Mrs. Loring states she believes in participatory management, in this case her plan appears to be too heavy-handed to work. Leaders at all levels must want to come up with missions. When it becomes a requirement, it can become a perfunctory assignment with no meaning. It is the position of the author that missions should come from inside leaders, not outside. They must reflect the needs (rewards) of the members of the group and provide vision beyond current goals. In some departments, this may not be possible. Therefore, to require each department manager to come up with a slogan may do more damage than good. The plan might work, however, on a volunteer basis. At least a few departments might create missions that would be meaningful. It is just not realistic to think this could happen in all departments.

The author defends Aaron and his balanced strategy. Only through the integration of all foundations into one's style will full benefits occur. Overemphasis of one or more foundations can be dangerous because of the interrelationships between all. Taking this stand, however, does not mean that Rose will not benefit. It is possible (not covered in the case) that Rose is already excellent at MRT and her decision-making capabilities are high. In this case she is filling in weak spots, and her strategy will work. For most people, however, Aaron's strategy is best.

CASE 17: EMPHASIS

Weaving the formula into one's style requires follow-through if success is to be achieved, so it would appear that Jill has a decided edge over Janice. People who make a big thing about behavioral changes often put on a good show but no permanent change takes place. This is a possibility with Janice. Jill's low-key approach may also offer benefits from a human-relations point of view. Her co-workers may not sense ahead of time that she is becoming a strong leader, so no negative or jealous waves from others may develop. The danger of coming on too strong is always present when behavioral changes are being made. Putting more leadership into your style should be a slow, sound, and permanent process for the best possible results.

CASE 18: PREDICTION

Answers to Self-Tests

CHAPTER 1

1. F (Psychologists have been unable to do this.)
2. F (Just the opposite. The higher you get the *more* opportunities there are—because so many potential leaders have fallen by the wayside.)
3. F (Coaches, ministers, military officers, and other leaders have also been involved.)
4. T (Most have used others as models, but have done it pretty much on their own.)
5. T (The success of one is sometimes dependent on the use of another.)
6. T (This is controversial but the author sticks with the basic premise.)
7. F (It is a vital part woven into all foundations.)
8. F (With their compassion for people they might find some parts easier.)
9. T
10. T (It is the contention of the author that the essence of leadership cannot be adequately explained in a single sentence or paragraph.)

CHAPTER 2

1. F
2. T
3. T
4. T (This is highly recommended.)
5. T
6. F (A primary advantage of the formula is that it can be used at all management levels.)
7. T
8. T (They would, however, be better leaders if they became better managers.)
9. T
10. T

CHAPTER 3

1. T
2. F   (Both are equally important.)
3. F
4. F
5. T
6. F   (The scale is only one signal. Besides, many successful leaders overcome early communication handicaps.)
7. T
8. F
9. T
10. F (Good communications skills are a foundation of the formula; management skills are a good background.)

CHAPTER 4

1. T
2. T   (This is a basic premise of the theory.)
3. T
4. F   (They provide too few and often the wrong ones.)
5. T   (This is a primary advantage of MRT.)
6. F   (The ultimate franchise to lead comes from followers.)
7. T
8. T
9. F   (Like anything else, it requires commitment and practice.)
10. T

CHAPTER 5

1. T   (This a very strong recommendation for MRT.)
2. T   (Too much structure or discipline without MRT can lower productivity instead of increasing it.)
3. F   (Role power comes from the position one occupies.)
4. T
5. F   (They often do not balance their knowledge power with their role and personality power.)

6. T

7. T

8. F (It is estimated that only about 10 percent of successful leaders have recognizable charisma.)

9. F (If the individual desires to become a leader, this should be a primary effort.)

10. T (Followers will recognize this sooner than most other efforts.)

CHAPTER 6

1. T

2. F

3. F

4. F (A prescribed, logical pattern is recommended, however.)

5. T

6. T

7. F (May produce a better decision, seldom faster.)

8. T

9. F

10. F (Lack of time forces many so-called gut decisions.)

CHAPTER 7

1. T

2. T

3. T (Some more than others, but some capacity is there.)

4. T

5. F (A positive force cannot be created without them.)

6. F (A two-level, two-way communications network is needed.)

7. F (The stronger the force, the less likely a counterforce will surface.)

8. F (All foundations are equally important.)

9. T

10. T

CHAPTER 8

1. F   (A mission is at a higher level, less practical, etc.)
2. F   (A mission helps create and sustain a positive force.)
3. T
4. T
5. T
6. T
7. F   (Articulation is usually the most difficult.)
8. F
9. T
10. T

CHAPTER 9

1. F   (It is a do-it-yourself project.)
2. F   (Strategy III is the most difficult and will probably produce greater results.)
3. F   (MRT, for example, can be applied in all human relationships.)
4. T
5. T
6. T   (At least one should be able to make a good start in adopting each of the five basic foundations.)
7. T
8. T   (This is especially true when it comes to applying more structure without MRT.)
9. T
10. T

Leadership Assessment Form

This form is provided for those who wish an easy but effective way to evaluate leaders on their application of the five leadership foundations. The form can be reproduced for use in classrooms, leadership seminars, and workshops.

On a scale of one to ten, rate each leader on the five foundations, then total the score at the bottom. If you rate a leader 40 or above, you are saying that the individual is an excellent leader; a score under 30 indicates a weak leader.

_____
(*name*)

Creating and maintaining a positive force.	10 9 8 7 6 5 4 3 2 1
Decision-making ability.	10 9 8 7 6 5 4 3 2 1
Maintenance of structure.	10 9 8 7 6 5 4 3 2 1
Application of MRT (reward systems).	10 9 8 7 6 5 4 3 2 1
Communication skills.	10 9 8 7 6 5 4 3 2 1

TOTAL _____

_____
(*name*)

Creating and maintaining a positive force.	10 9 8 7 6 5 4 3 2 1
Decision-making ability.	10 9 8 7 6 5 4 3 2 1
Maintenance of structure.	10 9 8 7 6 5 4 3 2 1
Application of MRT (reward systems).	10 9 8 7 6 5 4 3 2 1
Communication skills.	10 9 8 7 6 5 4 3 2 1

TOTAL _____

_____
(*name*)

Creating and maintaining a positive force.	10 9 8 7 6 5 4 3 2 1
Decision-making ability.	10 9 8 7 6 5 4 3 2 1
Maintenance of structure.	10 9 8 7 6 5 4 3 2 1
Application of MRT (reward systems).	10 9 8 7 6 5 4 3 2 1
Communication skills.	10 9 8 7 6 5 4 3 2 1

TOTAL _____

Leadership Communication Scale

Circle the number that best indicates where you fall in the scale, and enter the total in the space at the bottom.

I am constantly aware of my communication responsibilities.	10 9 8 7 6 5 4 3 2 1	I need to be reminded over and over about the importance of communication.
I understand fully the importance of nonverbal communication. I always project an outstanding visual image.	10 9 8 7 6 5 4 3 2 1	I constantly need to be reminded that there is such a thing as nonverbal communications. People must accept me the way I am.
I have learned how to keep my audience's attention when I talk to any size group.	10 9 8 7 6 5 4 3 2 1	The moment I start to talk I sense people are taking their minds elsewhere.
Rate me a 10 as a listener. I have developed all the skills and I practice them.	10 9 8 7 6 5 4 3 2 1	Give me a 1. I am a terrible listener.
I know how to adjust my conversation to the vocabulary and interest levels of others.	10 9 8 7 6 5 4 3 2 1	I always seem to be talking to myself.
I use appropriate voice control, diction, and delivery techniques.	10 9 8 7 6 5 4 3 2 1	I've given up on becoming even an average public speaker.
I seem to be able to pick just the right words to convey my message.	10 9 8 7 6 5 4 3 2 1	I'm clumsy with words. I'm always putting my foot in my mouth.
My messages are clear, concise, and extremely well received.	10 9 8 7 6 5 4 3 2 1	If I get any feedback at all, it is bad.
I never over- or under-talk; I'm always on target.	10 9 8 7 6 5 4 3 2 1	I either say too much or too little.
I instinctively know which media to use, and I fully employ all communications systems available.	10 9 8 7 6 5 4 3 2 1	Not only do I fail to use the right media, I do not take advantage of the opportunities available.

TOTAL _____

If you rated yourself 80 or above, you appear to possess outstanding communication skills. If you rated yourself between 60 and 80, you may be getting a signal that some improvement is necessary if you are to reach your leadership potential. If you rated yourself under 60, it would appear that substantial improvement is necessary.

Communications Survey Questionnaire

Dear co-worker, colleague, friend, or fellow student:

I have made a contract with myself to become a better communicator. I am asking you for assistance. Please complete the following survey, basing your ratings on the communications we have had in the past. First, rate me on both the listening and speaking scale (between 10, the best rating, and 1, the worst). Second, place a check in any box you think is applicable. Your criticisms will help me improve my skills. You are also encouraged to write out any suggestions for improvement not covered in the questionnaire.

Once you have finished, place this form in the envelope I have provided and seal it. I will, in turn, give your envelope (along with others) to a third person, who will provide me with a summary sheet. Your anonymity will be protected.

LISTENING SKILLS		SPEAKING SKILLS	
High 10 9 8 7 6 5 4 3 2 1 Low		**High** 10 9 8 7 6 5 4 3 2 1 Low	
Suggestions for improvement:		*Suggestions for improvement:*	
Refrain from interrupting so much.	☐	Speak more softly.	☐
Be less defensive when you reply.	☐	Speak with more authority.	☐
Slow your mind down so that you won't anticipate what I say before I say it.	☐	Speak more clearly.	☐
Let me know you are listening by more frequent eye contact.	☐	Speak less but say more.	☐
Improve your concentration.	☐	Put more excitement into your voice.	☐
Other suggestions: _____ _____		Other suggestions: _____ _____	

Communications Survey Questionnaire

Dear co-worker, colleague, friend, or fellow student:

I have made a contract with myself to become a better communicator. I am asking you for assistance. Please complete the following survey, basing your ratings on the communications we have had in the past. First, rate me on both the listening and speaking scale (between 10, the best rating, and 1, the worst). Second, place a check in any box you think is applicable. Your criticisms will help me improve my skills. You are also encouraged to write out any suggestions for improvement not covered in the questionnaire.

Once you have finished, place this form in the envelope I have provided and seal it. I will, in turn, give your envelope (along with others) to a third person, who will provide me with a summary sheet. Your anonymity will be protected.

LISTENING SKILLS	SPEAKING SKILLS
High 10 9 8 7 6 5 4 3 2 1 **Low**	**High** 10 9 8 7 6 5 4 3 2 1 **Low**
Suggestions for improvement:	*Suggestions for improvement:*
Refrain from interrupting so much. ☐	Speak more softly. ☐
Be less defensive when you reply. ☐	Speak with more authority. ☐
Slow your mind down so that you won't anticipate what I say before I say it. ☐	Speak more clearly. ☐
Let me know you are listening by more frequent eye contact. ☐	Speak less but say more. ☐
Improve your concentration. ☐	Put more excitement into your voice. ☐
Other suggestions: _____	Other suggestions: _____

Communications Survey Questionnaire

Dear co-worker, colleague, friend, or fellow student:

I have made a contract with myself to become a better communicator. I am asking you for assistance. Please complete the following survey, basing your ratings on the communications we have had in the past. First, rate me on both the listening and speaking scale (between 10, the best rating, and 1, the worst). Second, place a check in any box you think is applicable. Your criticisms will help me improve my skills. You are also encouraged to write out any suggestions for improvement not covered in the questionnaire.

Once you have finished, place this form in the envelope I have provided and seal it. I will, in turn, give your envelope (along with others) to a third person, who will provide me with a summary sheet. Your anonymity will be protected.

LISTENING SKILLS		SPEAKING SKILLS	
High 10 9 8 7 6 5 4 3 2 1 **Low**		**High** 10 9 8 7 6 5 4 3 2 1 **Low**	
Suggestions for improvement:		*Suggestions for improvement:*	
Refrain from interrupting so much.	☐	Speak more softly.	☐
Be less defensive when you reply.	☐	Speak with more authority.	☐
Slow your mind down so that you won't anticipate what I say before I say it.	☐	Speak more clearly.	☐
Let me know you are listening by more frequent eye contact.	☐	Speak less but say more.	☐
Improve your concentration.	☐	Put more excitement into your voice.	☐
Other suggestions: _____		Other suggestions: _____	

Acquisition Editor   Michael G. Crisp
Project Editor   Sara Boyd
Designer   Carol Harris
Illustrator/Cover Designer   Ralph Mapson
Compositor   Meredythe & Associates